KATA LEGRADY

KATA LEGRADY

SKIRA

Edited by
David Rosenberg

Cover
Government Balançoir, 2011
Synthetic resin, metal lacquered,
original saddle (Hermès, orange)
153 × 237 × 37 cm

Art director
Marcello Francone

Design
Luigi Fiore

Editorial coordination
Vincenza Russo

Copy editor
Emanuela Di Lallo

Layout
Fayçal Zaouali

Photographs
Antonio Maniscalco

First published in Italy in 2013 by
Skira Editore S.p.A.
Palazzo Casati Stampa
via Torino 61
20123 Milano
Italy
www.skira.net

Printed and bound in Italy. First edition

ISBN: 978-88-572-1965-3

Distributed in USA, Canada, Central &
South America by Rizzoli International
Publications, Inc., 300 Park Avenue
South, New York, NY 10010, USA.
Distributed elsewhere in the world
by Thames and Hudson Ltd., 181A High
Holborn, London WC1V 7QX, United
Kingdom.

Contents

Kata Legrady's Art of War

Standing before Kata Legrady's works one would feel inclined to say that weapons are the horizon of her exploration. In fact, army bombs are her favourite subject. And yet, it is obvious that Kata isn't fond of real weapons, the ones used in war to kill and destroy. She feels powerless, like every common mortal, when faced with the devastating military power circulating in the contemporary world. And since she doesn't want to forgo her steadfast opposition to it, she does what every good artist should do. She exploits her own weapons, which are and have always been imagination, creativity and irony, to deprive of any meaning the function of real weapons, presenting them to the viewer this time sublimated by a precise and aseptic, aestheticizing and ironic formalization, capable of recuperating a different function, one that can be playful and even hilarious at times. A perfect example of this is the exhibition she has prepared for our Foundation, where lethal anti-tank mines are morphed into huge wild daisies. Where powerful intercontinental missiles are covered – in a singular cross-contamination with the hippie culture from the mid-1960s – in flowers, butterflies and big hearts. Where a Beretta revolver perfectly reproduced at a scale of 100:1 becomes an unusual but apparently delightful children's rocking horse, while a destructive bomb in an unlikely fuchsia colour is merely an aesthetic, almost ornamental object. The ornament, which can consist of Smarties or colours that look as though they've been taken from a Pantone for makeup, becomes the vehicle of the perturbing effect that, apart from distancing itself from the basic object, turns it in the direction of a new conceptual horizon, with a final result that is capable of combining emotional coldness and conceptual elegance, compositional clarity and ironic bewilderment. This way, with the weapons of her art and those alone, which truly deserve to be preserved, Kata Legrady deconstructs and attempts to transform the tragic reality that today, just as in the past, fills the newspapers and the TV news, offering us, by explicit throw-backs to childhood and Walt Disney, another world that is apparently more naive and, at the same time, more intriguing. It is a direct invitation to rediscover purity, candour and the amazement of a lost day and age and world where weapons, real ones this time, are no longer weapons but beautiful toys whose sole purpose is play.

Gino Di Maggio

Kata Legrady at the Mudima

Created in Milan by Gino Di Maggio in 1988, the Fondazione Mudima is a unique place of its kind: an interdisciplinary space devoted above all to artists "who shift the boundaries between arts, who build bridges between the visual arts, literature, music and the new media". Mudima reflects the personality of both its founder and director and of its city. On the one hand, we have Gino Di Maggio, an art lover and writer, a great collector and scholar of the Fluxus movement; on the other, Milan, a city moulded by history and the omnipresence of art, design and fashion, described by Filippo Tommaso Marinetti in his day as "traditional and Futurist" at the same time. Since it opened, the Fondazione Mudima has organized shows by many artists of very different horizons, including Allan Kaprow, Yoko Ono, Daniel Spoerri, Nam June Paik, Marcel Duchamp, César, Arman, Piero Manzoni, Ben Vautier, Joseph Beuys, Takako Saito, Ben Patterson, Milan Knižák, Sandro Chia, Lee Ufan, Kazuo Shiraga and Shim Moon Seup, which have very often given rise to specific works and projects. Not to mention memorable concerts by musicians such as John Cage, La Monte Young and Giuseppe Chiari as well as significant extramural projects. It is impossible to sum up the activities of this simultaneously remarkable and self-effacing place in just a few lines.

It is certainly no coincidence that the *genius loci* brought about contact between the Fondazione Mudima and Kata Legrady, who worked for a long time in the field of classical music and trained as an opera singer before devoting herself to the plastic arts. The catalogue tells the story of this meeting and this first Mudima solo show of work by Kata Legrady, an artist who also works in her own way on the boundaries between the various creative fields.
An exhibition is also a way to interweave the views, questions and dialogues to which it gives rise. This is what happens here with the contributions of two outstanding figures, Arturo Schwarz and Bazon Brock, who each present a scholarly and sensitive assessment of Kata Legrady's work. We are most grateful to them both.
Kata Legrady addresses and melds normally separate universes. Immediately striking with its images of weapons, candies, toys and masks, this catalogue is aimed to explore what is hiding behind the "evidence" of Kata's work: to explore what this evidence encloses and conceals.

David Rosenberg
Paris, July 2013

Kata Legrady:
Innocence Rediscovered

Arturo Schwarz

The artistic itinerary of Kata Legrady confirms Lautréamont's assertion that art "must be made by all and not by one".[1] We can recall the fact that Kata, before concentrating on art, wanted to become a soprano and had studied from 1989 to 1993 at the Conservatory of Pécs, Hungary. Through an odd coincidence, whereas Kata was by origin a daughter of Melpomene, the Muse of Singing, Daniel Spoerri (author of the text cited *infra*) is a son of Terpsichore – the Muse of Dance. I remember that his career began as *primo ballerino* in the classical ballet company of the State Theatre of Bern. Daniel (who had his first solo show in my gallery in 1961) speaks of their initial vocation in a text where he praises the perfection of her work: "You too, Kata, have been blessed by heavenly favor, as I am. You too have never spent time in art academies; they have never instructed you on how to paint or draw. And then, all of a sudden, without any foreplay, any trials, you find yourself with a work of your own – and it is perfect".[2]

But how do we know when we are in the presence of a work that can legitimately be called "art"? In my view, the answer is quite simple. Such a work should possess three essential qualities – precisely those qualities that can be found in the work of Kata Legrady.

The first of these characteristics is originality, which is indispensable to give the work the capacity to expand our visual and mental perspectives. But originality on its own will not suffice. In our technological age it is relatively easy to come up with exciting novelties that soon become obsolete, when other newer ones appear. That which is truly original and unique brings with it the promise of timeless validity. The imaginative power of artists has developed to such a degree that they are able to create a hitherto unknown reality. This implies that they cannot create "on commission", following the orders of a client. Instead, the artists obey a demanding inner impulse. This independence brings us to the second quality of the artwork.

In fact, if an artwork has to be the result of an impelling cognitive and emotional need, it must take the advice given by

Polonius to his son Laertes: "This above all: to thine own self be true" (*Hamlet* I: 3). But again, the sole dictate of authenticity is not enough. The creative impulse is not only a prerogative of artists; a mentally deranged person may feel the same need, and while the resulting work can at times possess expressive power and aesthetic value, this is not always the case. The second quality demanded of the artist is that his or her *different* creation be controlled by an equally demanding intellect.

The third quality is the most elusive, either to describe or to achieve. The artwork should not only reveal a new reality to us and be the result of an inner existential necessity; it should also prompt a sentiment of an initiatic character, and emanate a poetic aura. The great poet Pierre Reverdy once told me that "poetry is an emotion", and I would say that the same applies to art. Roman Jacobson wrote, "The object of the literary scene is not literature, but literarity, meaning that which gives any work a literary quality".[3] Likewise, if I look at a work of art, I am interested not so much in its aesthetic qualities as in its emotional and poetic value that gives it an artistic dimension. This quality is ineffable. Art, like poetry, contains an element of mystery that should not be allowed to dissipate, if the work is to have a lasting impact.

In his *Critique of Judgement* Kant provides an epistemological basis for the three rules outlined above. He observes that "fine arts must necessarily be regarded as arts of *genius*"[4] and goes on to observe that genius "is a talent for producing that for which no definite rule can be given; it is not a mere aptitude for what can be learnt by a rule. Hence *originality* must be its first property".[5] He also specifies that given the fact that "original nonsense" can exist, the genius must produce works that are "models, i.e. *exemplary*; and they consequently ought not to spring from imitation, but must serve as a standard or rule of judgement for others" (ibid.). Kant, finally, hints at the ineffable nature of an artwork and its essentially unconscious origin when he states that "the author of a product for which he is indebted to his genius does not himself know how he has come by his Ideas; and he has not the power to devise the like at pleasure or in accordance with a plan, and to communicate it to others in precepts that will enable them to produce similar products" (ibid.).

Regarding the third golden rule, which states that an artwork must have a poetic dimension, Kant, defining spirit (*Geist*) in the aesthetic sense as the "vivifying principle of the soul",[6] explicitly states that an aspiring artwork "without spirit" cannot achieve the status of art. He concludes his analysis with a formula, saying that "beautiful art, then, requires *imagination, intellect, spirit and taste*".[7] To put it another way, using the words of Kandinsky, "Beauty is something that comes from an inner psychic need. Beauty is something that is beautiful inside, that springs from the soul and 'enriches' the soul".[8]

But the art world, today, is going through a situation of dual, deadly ambiguity. With the excuse of rejecting the formalism of art *for* art, a form of art *against* art has emerged. A new, self-appointed avant-garde has all the characteristics of the most hackneyed academicism: repetition of identical things, in terms of both theme and form; recourse to the monumental and the boundless; an accent on decoration; the ambition to raise eyebrows at all costs; a total lack of authentic inspiration.

A totally unprecedented semantic confusion reigns. Genres that certainly have their own artistic dignity but have nothing to do with Hegel's definition of "plastic art" are grouped into just that category. For example, happenings are simply improvisations (as in jazz) of mini-theatre. I remember being present at some of the first happenings in 1960 in New York; Allan Kaprow, Claes Oldenburg, John Cage and Jim Dine agreed that this medium of expression should be defined as a "theatrical event without a pre-set plot". Likewise, video belongs to the category of film-making; installations to set design; works made with neon tubes are examples of interior decoration; Body Art is the expression of extreme narcissism, often with a sado-masochistic bent – in the best of cases, we might define Body Art as a form of theatre.

* * *

I think the work of Kata Legrady stands out for four fundamental traits. Let's list them. Her creative praxis is determined, to a great extent, by her unconscious; then, the work has a playful dimension; she uses, in an utterly personal way, the "readymade" in the Duchampian sense of the term; finally, she observes the world with a gaze that has conserved the innocence, curiosity and inventiveness of childhood. Prior to examining each of these characteristics, I would like to make some preliminary considerations.

Let's approach the first distinctive feature of Kata's work, i.e. the importance of the unconscious in the creative process. In one of his dazzling fragments, Novalis declares: "Poetry is reality, the true, absolute reality".[9] Little more than one century later, two verses of Apollinaire almost echo this statement: "You read the flyers catalogues posters that shout out / There's the morning's poetry and as for prose there are the newspapers".[10] I suspect that for Novalis, "absolute reality" also and above all included that sunken, obscure zone of the self that dictated to him his most enlightening thoughts; just as for Apollinaire visual material served only to reawaken the emotions buried in the treasure trove of the unconscious. A remark of Apollinaire would seem to bear this out, when he writes "the great poets have been 'hearers', not seers". Instead, I would say that – like artists – they are both hearers and seers. In fact, they have been hearers, and very attentive ones too, but the voice they listened to was the one that rose from the depths of being. Rimbaud understood this, and demanded that the poet become a seer. Like the Pythia of Delphi, the poet then finds the word-oracles – or more precisely the verse-oracles – that are striking due to their illuminating power. Just as the artist must "become a seer" to discover the submerged dimension of the model to be brought to light.

We should specify that when she develops her works Kata retraces – totally unconsciously, of course – the steps of the *longissima via* that leads the Artist (as the first alchemists called themselves) to enlightenment, on the level, that is, where art is no longer utopia but becomes initiation, self-awareness. The artist then achieves a state of *clairvoyance*, in keeping with Rimbaud's imperative. This happens because the artist is inspired, possessed by a creative stimulus of a trans-personal and trans-rational character. In fact, as Plato teaches, "no one achieves true and inspired divination when in their rational mind".[11] So it is worth repeating that when we find elements in her work that come from the treasure trove of the collective unconscious, Kata is unaware of the symbolic value of the iconographic motifs and schemes she has used. They are chosen in response to unconscious impulses even though, at the start, the goal was to consciously express the theme set by the title of the work. As in any authentic work of art, "conscious memory" and "unconscious memory"[12] go hand in hand, in what Duchamp called "a little game between 'I' and 'me'".[13] After all, Kata herself is well aware that what determines the work is precisely this "unconscious memory", fruit of the collective unconscious: in fact, she confessed to David Rosenberg that the meaning of her art "is buried in the depths, the layers of an existence that has nothing to do with us".[14]

André Breton believed poetry to be "all inner adventure", specifying that it was the only adventure that interested him.[15] The adventure of the artist is no different. Both artist and poet have the task of exploring that "all inner" realm of the unconscious where they are able to see a parlour "at the bottom of a lake".[16] Recalling the words of Rimbaud, "it is wrong to say: I think. One ought to say: I am thought", the theorist of Surrealism noted that "ever more acute and invasive … is the sensation of being moved, or even to say of being *played*, by forces beyond our own".[17] In art – and Surrealism is the demonstration of this – the poet, like the artist, treads the path towards the unconscious with motivations that are the opposite of those of the psychoanalyst. While the artist probes the unconscious to become clairvoyant and creative, the psychoanalyst brings it to light for therapeutic aims.

Nevertheless, they have something in common: the poet, the artist and the psychoanalyst strive for an *other* form of knowledge.

I have mentioned the importance of the factor of play in Kata's *poiesis*. Play – besides representing a way of being and a philosophy of life – is seen here in the sense assigned by Johan Huizinga to this activity in his fundamental *Homo Ludens* in 1938. For the Dutch historian play forms the basis for any culture. For Schiller play is an activity that cannot be eliminated from human nature. Play pursues no objective other than itself, and it is driven by no precise rational purpose. It is an act where sensibility and rationality coexist in the playful action, making man free,[18] offering an escape from the demands of the reality principle. Hilde Hein explains, "the theories that emphasize the formal element of play are also predicated on its non-reality. … The sole fact that it possesses this quality in common with aesthetic activity and, perhaps, with a certain number of other activities validates the project of exploring one in terms of the other".[19] Maybe we should emphasize the fact that in the future golden age envisioned by Marx and Engels, when man will have solved the problems of social and ideological alienation and will be free to devote himself to poetic and artistic activities with the same capacity he would invest in productive ones, art will finally take on a playful dimension: "In a communist society there are no painters but only people who engage in painting among other activities".[20] Then, as Trotsky imagined, "The average human type will rise to the heights of an Aristotle, a Goethe, or a Marx. And above this ridge new peaks will rise".[21]

On the "readymade" of Duchamp, let's first of all examine certain constants that are found in Kata's objects. They are non-functional and arbitrary; they do not blend in a reality they intend to discredit; they are subjective, given the fact that they embody the wishes of the artist, and in doing so reveal archetypal desires shared by all human beings, just as the analysis of dreams reveals the archetypal meaning of the symbols that populate them. In Freudian terms, Kata's works, like dreams, are the masked expression of repressed desires. For her, the objects serve first of all to "compose a portrait of a reality that is never directly depicted or represented … [the objects] are always disguised by what symbolizes them".[22]

An English poet in the twentieth century wrote a poem, a few lines of which have remained imprinted in my memory for over seventy years (I am now 89): "A poor life this / If full of care / We have no time / To stand and stare". William Henry Davies – that was the name of the poet – was quoting, probably without knowing it, a sentence from the Tabula Smaragdina that urges us to discover the beauty that is there before our eyes, under our feet, within reach of those rare, lucky beings – like Kata Legrady – who are capable of noticing it.

Having said this, we can observe that Marcel Duchamp was the first artist who put the precept of the Tabula Smaragdina into practice, discovering the beauty of a simple manmade thing – the "readymade". But to avoid facile imitations we should also recall that he indicated certain conditions that govern the process leading to the transformation of a common object into an artwork. First of all, the object has to be "disoriented", namely re-presented in a context that is different from its usual setting, with the goal of "decontextualizing" it (like the *Bicycle Wheel* of 1913 which is mounted on a kitchen stool). This is true of Kata's objects, which are in fact "disoriented": as she once told David Rosenberg, they "seem to float between heaven and earth. They float in the space of the gallery or in the space of representation, like icons or divinities".[23] Furthermore, the object must also have a title, "a verbal colour" which, for Duchamp, does not have to be descriptive, but should transport the mind towards a precise mental region. For a snow shovel, for example, he invented the title *In Advance of the Broken Arm.* We should remember that for Kata, too, the "disoriented" objects take on a new verbal identity; for example, a grenade is called *Pineapple* (see the works of 2009–10); a bomb gets the title *Little Boy*, and so on.

Finally, we have reached the third element of the *poiesis* of Kata – her way of *looking at* the world. She has conserved the gaze of childhood, still capable of wonder, of knowing the difference between *looking* and *seeing.* She looks at a reality that may seem banal or even ugly to almost everyone, and she sees (or discovers), with the third eye of the poet, a beauty she transmutes into artistic reality. On this subject, we can recall the case of Hans Arp. This protagonist of the historical avant-garde had an extraordinary personality – the wisdom of an elder, the fingers of a magician, the eyes and capacity for wonder of a child. I would like to narrate an episode I experienced myself, regarding the childlike gaze he directed, like Kata, at the world. I owned one of his sculptures, entitled *The Idol of the Rabbits.* Not one of my many visitors ever saw any resemblance to a rabbit in this work. One day the 7-year-old son of a friend came to visit. As soon as he saw the sculpture, he exclaimed "what a nice rabbit!" The phrase of Deleuze then came to mind: "Art allows us to become children again", and I would add that only an authentic artist knows how to obey the power of the childlike imagination.

There is another constant that sets Kata's work apart – from the *Guns and Candies* of 2008, to the *Gasmasks* of 2009, *Little Boy* in 2009 and 2010, and the more recent works she made in 2011: *Mickey, Pearl Harbor*; *Government Balançoir*; *Catwoman*; *Cheval à bascule*, all the way to the *Disney* series. This constant is humour. We all know that humour has a tragic nature; it marks a moment of absolute independence of poetry and it is above all a revolt of the spirit and the unconscious against the conditionings of society and life. Humour has a boundless virtue of defiance and provocation. It is a masterfully subversive factor of opposition, since it consecrates the triumph of the pleasure principle over the reality principle. Thus, with Kata, an artillery shell (see her grenades), a bomb, a pistol, a Kalashnikov can be transformed from devices of death to works of art.

I would like to conclude these thoughts with the lucid words of David Rosenberg, who finds in the works of Kata "our desire for lightness, or our irrepressible need to eroticize the real that masks, without completely concealing them, our most visceral fears".[24]

1. Lautréamont, "Poésies II" (1870), in *Lautréamont. Œuvres complètes* (Paris: La Pléiade and Gallimard, 2009), p. 288. I have shifted the quote from poetry to art, conserving the intent.

2. "Dear Kata Legrady", in *Bombs and Candies* (Milan: Skira, 2011), p. 7.

3. Roman Jakobson, *Huit questions de poétique* [1921] (Paris: Points-Seuil, 1977), p. 16.

4. Immanuel Kant, *Critique of Judgement*, 1790.

5. Ibid.

6. Ibid.

7. Ibid.

8. Wassily Kandinsky, *Concerning the Spiritual in Art*, 1912.

9. Novalis, *Pollen and Fragments* (Grand Rapids, Michigan: Phanes Press, September 1989).

10. Guillaume Apollinaire, "Zone" [1912], in *Alcools* [1913], in *Œuvres poétiques* (Paris: Gallimard, 1959), p. 39.

11. *Timaeus*, xxxii: 72e.

12. Regarding these two categories, see the contribution of Eric R. Kandel, neuroscientist and Nobel Prize for Biology 2000.

13. "Marcel Duchamp", interview in *The Artist's Voice*, edited by Katharine Kuh (New York: Harper & Row, 1962), p. 83.

14. David Rosenberg, "War is Over", in *Bombs and Candies* 2011, p. 16.

15. André Breton, "Entretien avec Madeleine Chaptal" [1962], in *Perspective cavalière* (Paris: Gallimard, 1970), p. 211.

16. André Breton, *Le Surréalisme et la peinture* [1928] (Paris: Gallimard, 1966), p. 5.

17. André Breton, *L'Art magique*, 1957.

18. Friedrich Schiller, *Über die ästhetische Erziehung des Menschen*, 1795.

19. Hilde Hein, "Play as an Aesthetic Concept", in *The Journal of Aesthetics and Art Criticism* (Wayne), xxvii, no. 1 (Fall 1968), pp. 70–71.

20. Cfr. Karl Marx and Friedrich Engels, *The German Ideology*, 1846.

21. Leon Trotsky, *Literature and Revolution* [1924] (New York: Russell & Russell, 1957).

22. David Rosenberg, "Le piège du miroir", in *Kata Legrady,* catalogue of the exhibition at Galerie Rabouan Moussion, Paris, p. 2.

23. Ibid.

24. Ibid., p. 3.

Dulce et Decorum:
The Candy-coated Weaponry
of Kata Legrady.
An Experimental Contribution
to Cultural History

Bazon Brock

The highest German design prize, "Good Form", has been awarded by the Federal Government since 1969. For decades the jury consisted of first-class theorists, designers, directors of institutes and art historians. After the war, the programme of re-education in West Germany, which was also required to advance the concept of "good form", was to subsequently erase from design and architectural history any remembrance of its alliance with the fascists and national socialists, as well as with the communist progressives. However, in the 1970s it could no longer be denied that futurists, Bauhaus artists and the glorious Russian Vkhutemas guys had been in substantial proximity to these said worldviews. One could no longer conceal that even Mies van der Rohe in 1936, indeed even after the closure of the Bauhaus in Berlin, realized Nazi-controlled *Zeitgeist* exhibitions. Artists of the so-called "German inwardness", such as Emil Nolde, considered themselves amongst the true national socialists, before (beginning in 1937) they had to suffer as "degenerates", prohibited from working, sent to prison, or worse.

Considering that in the young Federal Republic such entanglements could not be aptly explained by the greatest minds such as Gottfried Benn, Carl Schmitt, Ernst Jünger and Martin Heidegger through "saving the world" type policies, they rather contented themselves with the simple task of sorting according to "good" or "evil", "peaceful" or "aggressive", "cumulative" or "destructive". In the field of design that meant that weapons should never be rewarded for their "good shape", despite the fact that they seemingly met all the design criteria of modernity – such as forgoing ornamentation, a reduction to only elementary and primary forms according to the motto of "less is more", in which the "truth to the material" is fulfilled to the highest degree.

During the time in which Lucius Burckhardt was chairman of the German Werkbund, his intent was to oppose the lazy thinking and the morally-fuelled discussions in order to finally confront "good form" with the reality of designerly high performance. He placed a Heckler & Koch weapon between other objects, such as a Hans Hollein tea and coffee service or imitations of the earlier Wagenfeld or Marianne Brandt designs. Since Burckhardt was a member of the jury, he was also allowed to provide detailed justification for the product proposal. This succeeded so convincingly that the jurors had to recognize that the weapon design had earned the highest award; however, this honour would have been completely politically incorrect. A solution to the conflict could not be found, and the prize was not awarded for many years.

Incidentally, the aforementioned service by Hans Hollein in plated silver had the design appearance of an aircraft carrier. It was first a post-modern typically visionary element, even a caricature, but rather tended to be seen as serious fun: in order to maintain their mental stability during times of stress – considering the responsibility of warfare – generals and admirals would carry private valuables in their baggage. Russian commissioners were surprised when they listed the items from captured German generals in that the objects that served to comfort the mind were items that would usually be reserved for the likes of noblemen.

American military commanders were not far behind the German mindset. To celebrate the first successful H-bomb testing at Bikini, Navy admirals required that the celebration cake was made in the shape of a typical blast fungus served only on the finest dishes – with the First Lady of the Admiralty as a secondary figure in which a cap in the form of an already diminishing mushroom cloud was placed on her head.

Shortly before Burkhardt blighted the federal prize "Good Form", another truly magical alliance of war and cakes in Vienna had formed. With the help of the ruling social democrats, who were rewarded with treats every week, the young Udo Proksch bought the k.u.k. Hofzuckerbäckerei Demel. This central European institute of confectionery art used to decorate the shop windows of the establishment at the Kohlmarkt with contemporary pop-art style arrangements of candy and chocolate.

Proksch was an academically trained artist, a *Zeitgeist* entrepreneur and social *filou*. He had heard of Burckhardt's "design is invisible" theory and came upon the grand idea of using conceptual art to demonstrate that the political confectioners such as himself point to a reality that should be rendered invisible through the shop window decoration. As an artist on a reconnaissance mission, he decided to reveal the beauty-substantiated truth – in a *salto mortale*. He became involved in the international arms trade, in which he invited the appropriate clients to the Demel, in order to beguile them with tartlets. He was one ahead of the Hollein design pretence – indeed he did not design a warship, but rather bought a discarded ship that he loaded with heavy weapons, and which was subsequently sunk for reasons of insurance.

The tragedy of his rationale was similar to the present-day art forgery processes. Proksch's conceptual artwork was held for a forgery with the intent to obtain a substantial insurance claim. It was supposed, as is customary with artists, to only deal with fictions, to have loaded the ship with dummies instead of real weapons. The wise Proksch believed to be on the safe side, as his ship was thought to be lost in the depths of the Indian Ocean. Hatred of the artist's genius didn't allow his duped "friends" to rest. They developed expensive technologies for deep-sea salvage in order to dispel the artistic fictionality. The costs significantly exceeded the insured amount – but a pretentious critic of the political confectioner Zuckerbäckerei had repaid his malicious joke.

Caesar's political-philosophical analysis was that "cruel people like to eat sweets"; Caesar therefore surrounded himself with obese men, because their weight was close to the size of their sugar consumption, and thus their cerebral activity – because sugar is the basic substance of the brain activation and mainly promotes the basic functions of the psyche such as the assertiveness as measured aggression or self-gratification as a mechanism of stimulatory feedback effect.

Relevant studies show that the aforementioned overweightness is, in the meantime, given as a directive from the top tiers in the gang culture of the lower social strata. The average weight of today's motorcycle gangsters corresponds to that of Caesar's advisors; these strong men needed such an aggressive presence and self-indulgence rites in order to assert themselves against the legal criminals.

Whoever has had the pleasure of aesthetically examining desserts offered by highway rest stop service areas – the favourite restaurants of the big guys – knows, finally, why the Latin *dulce*, which denoted the satisfaction at the death for the fatherland, has subsequently become the Italian *dolce*, a term for sweets and desserts. Statistics prove that American death row inmates request a last meal in which a large portion consists of desserts. In this example, it is evident that there exists a connection between the childlike calming of the need for love and the imminent death.

It is precisely this context that Kata Legrady has dedicated to her works – that I'd rather like to call implements of knowledge or theoretical objects, because they are played down if I designate them as "artworks". It touches on the ridiculous or a certain arrogance to want to refer to Seurat, Picabia, Polke, to Lichtenstein and Damien Hirst and their use of grid images or serial dot shapes. The supposed compliment, to extol something a work of art, is turned into malicious joy through the inappropriateness of the comparison. Shouldn't be forbidden – in the face of armed violence, financial capital as the firepower of fundamentalist terror or murderous cancer – to still maintain that art is the highest measure of the importance of human acts and at the same time propagate "anything goes art"?

Compared to this art-deification, abnormal advertisements or the fashion design attitude-passepartouts are still a downright enlightening force. On such realities Kata Legrady orientates her works more so than at such major artists, and it serves the highest intellectual glory in that she evades the commitment to absolute contemporaneity by letting herself not be seduced to adapt to mandatory success-enforcing artists' roles. She surrenders herself to the acknowledgement that any garbage collector is more important for the functioning of a society, than all the artists put together. Because even if the artist had the idea to strike, nobody would notice, but if the garbage collectors strike, in no later than in ten days social life would collapse. And Kata is a garbage collector working against today's art waste production.

The prefix "Kata" in Greek, the language of our basic conceptualization, refers to transformations (i.e. metamorphosis) of conditions. How does that work? Perhaps it is through the development of complementary circumstances such as this world and the hereafter, or earthly and heavenly life and death. We do not intend that the transformation of life into death can take place in the same way as that of mortality into immortality, which is of course what is meant with "dulce et decorum est pro patria mori." Because the most satisfactory (*dulce*) is to die for the fatherland, if indeed, their contemporaries promise never to forget the fallen or rather those killed in action.

All Sunday artists claim immortality by insisting that dying for the fatherland is equivalent to living for their art. But probably what is rather meant is the life of the art, and since few people are privileged to this practice, the artist-individualist masses feel sentenced to a social death.

The psychology of exclusion, rejection and contempt, which the artists maintain to increase their self-consciousness, is subject to a fundamental mistake: failure is simply not a sign of great ideas, therefore rejection is not the recognition of the unrecognizable meaning of the works. This ideology characterizes the "art-making process" as a confection. Here Legrady proves to be an ideology critic in the best European tradition. The general "art posturing" wants to enforce authenticity, to propagate self-actualization, to expose errors and break through viewing habits. But it applies just exactly to criticize this smug claim to truth.

Where truth, goodness and beauty cannot be dogmatically asserted, only the liar saves the truth – in that admitting the falsity indicates that the confessor still knows something of the truth. The recognized failures of the arts as that recognized falsity as such is still true. Kata Legrady therefore has not produced artworks, but rather insights into the untenable nature of the work's claim. In this sense she is a confident granddaughter of Orson Welles, who with *F for Fake* in 1974 was able to expand the cultural history into a decisive dimension – faking is indeed not forgery.

Rather than to stick art forgers in prison, you should make them into professors, so that they give the young people the dignity of the recognized falsehood. Faking is not a criminal act but rather an act of enlightenment about the inevitability of the work with the identified falsehood.

It is precisely in this spirit that I confess that I take the work of Kata Legrady seriously, as a sign of unyielding insistence on the power of the confession and an appreciation of the acknowledged falsity. And in doing so, I'm an old-fashioned eccentric. Eccentrics were those humane gentlemen, that is, the truly civilized people of the eighteenth century, when a precursor of Legrady's theoretical objects as an expression of sophistication of *dulce* and *dolce* was invented: "the void" – such as a pastry made from beaten egg whites (like the French meringue), which is shared after a meal in a specially designated place for that kind of indulgence, an exercise in devotion to the "almost nothing", in the bubble-like void, like sipping a divine demon interstellar manna and ambrosia.

I use Legrady's sugar weapons as such "voids". They stimulate me to intellectual pleasure as a sensuality of the mind, and I do not expect more of the objects than what I am able to achieve. What more can an artist hope for?

Kata Legrady
Fondazione Mudima, Milan, 2011

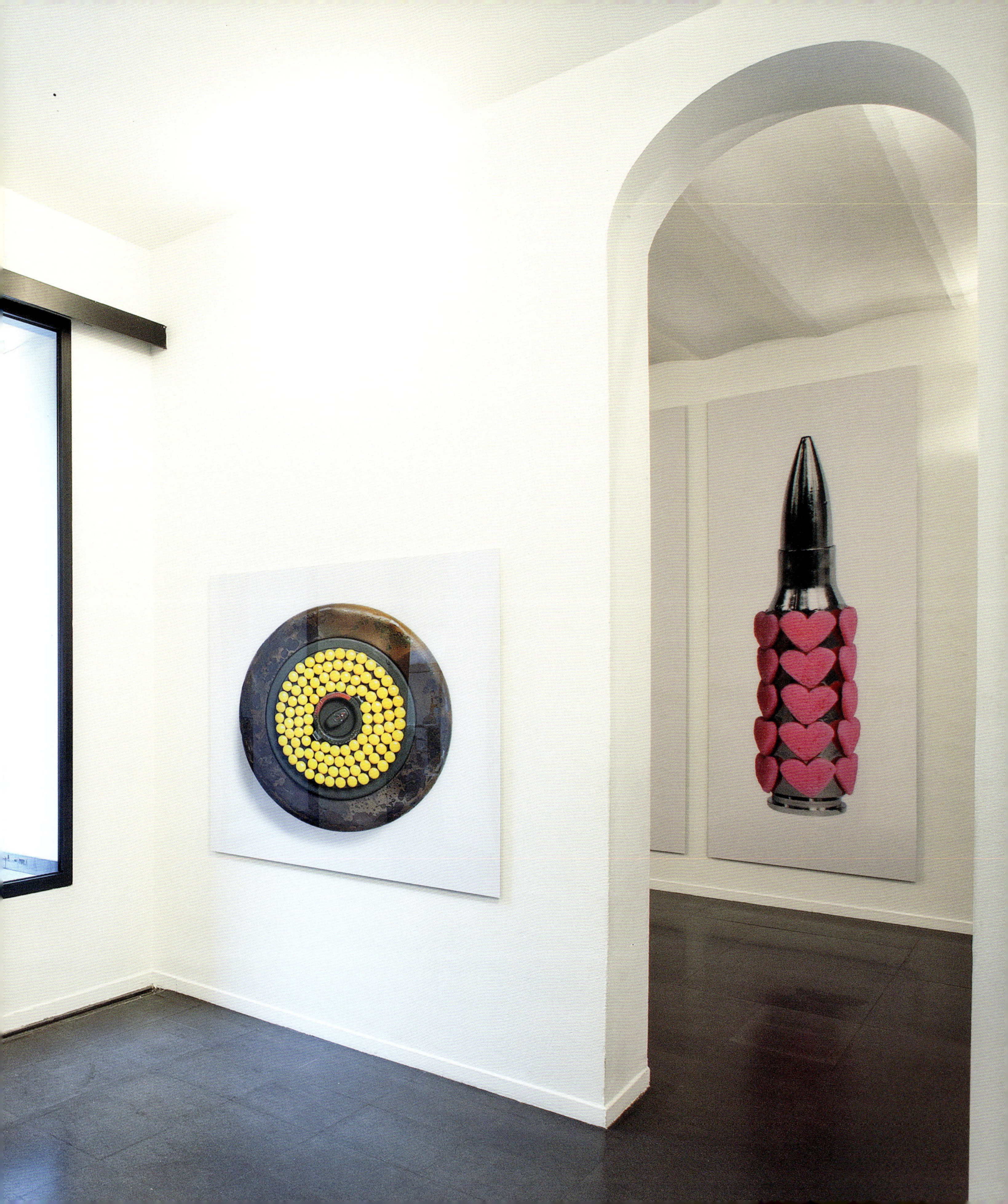

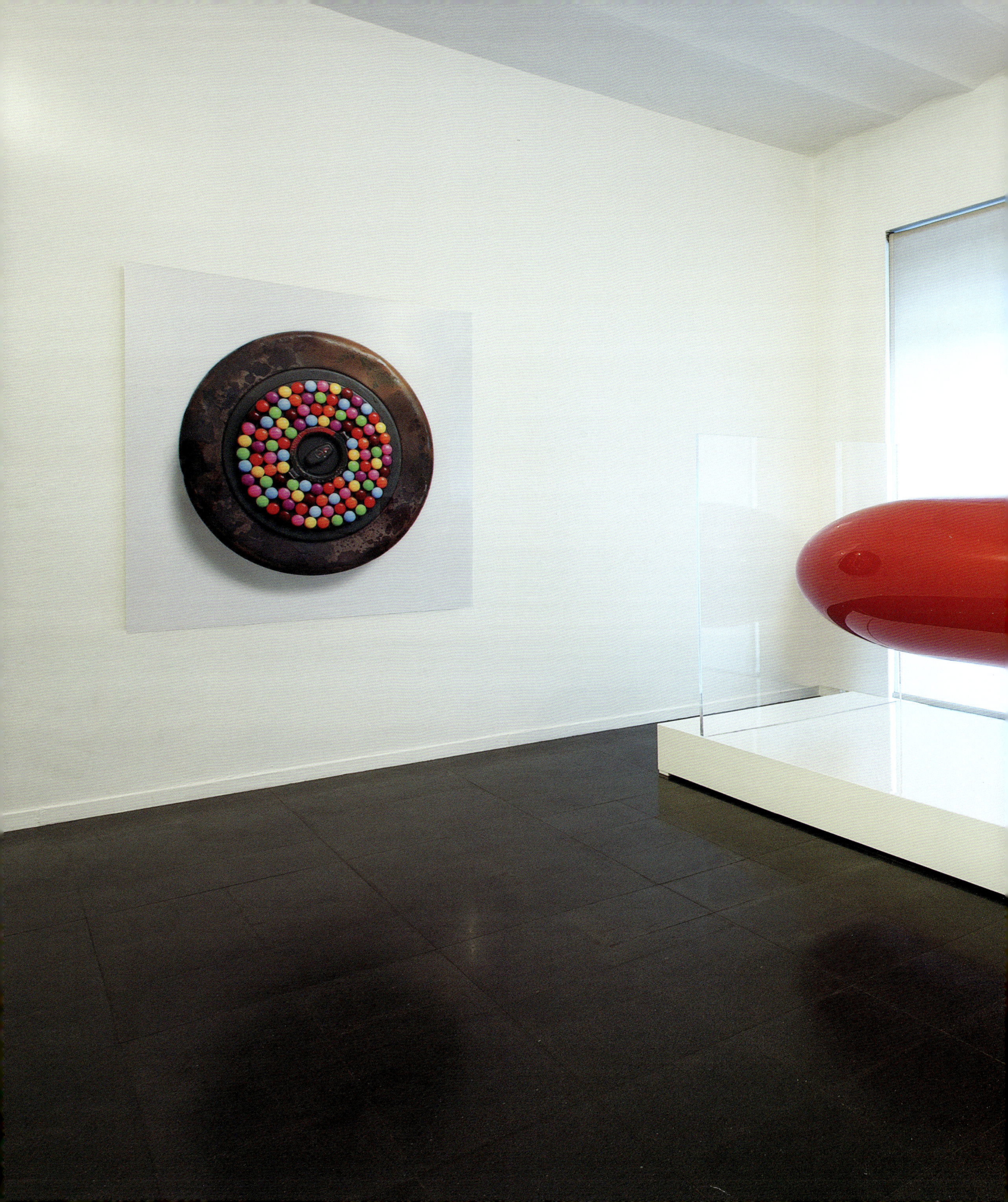

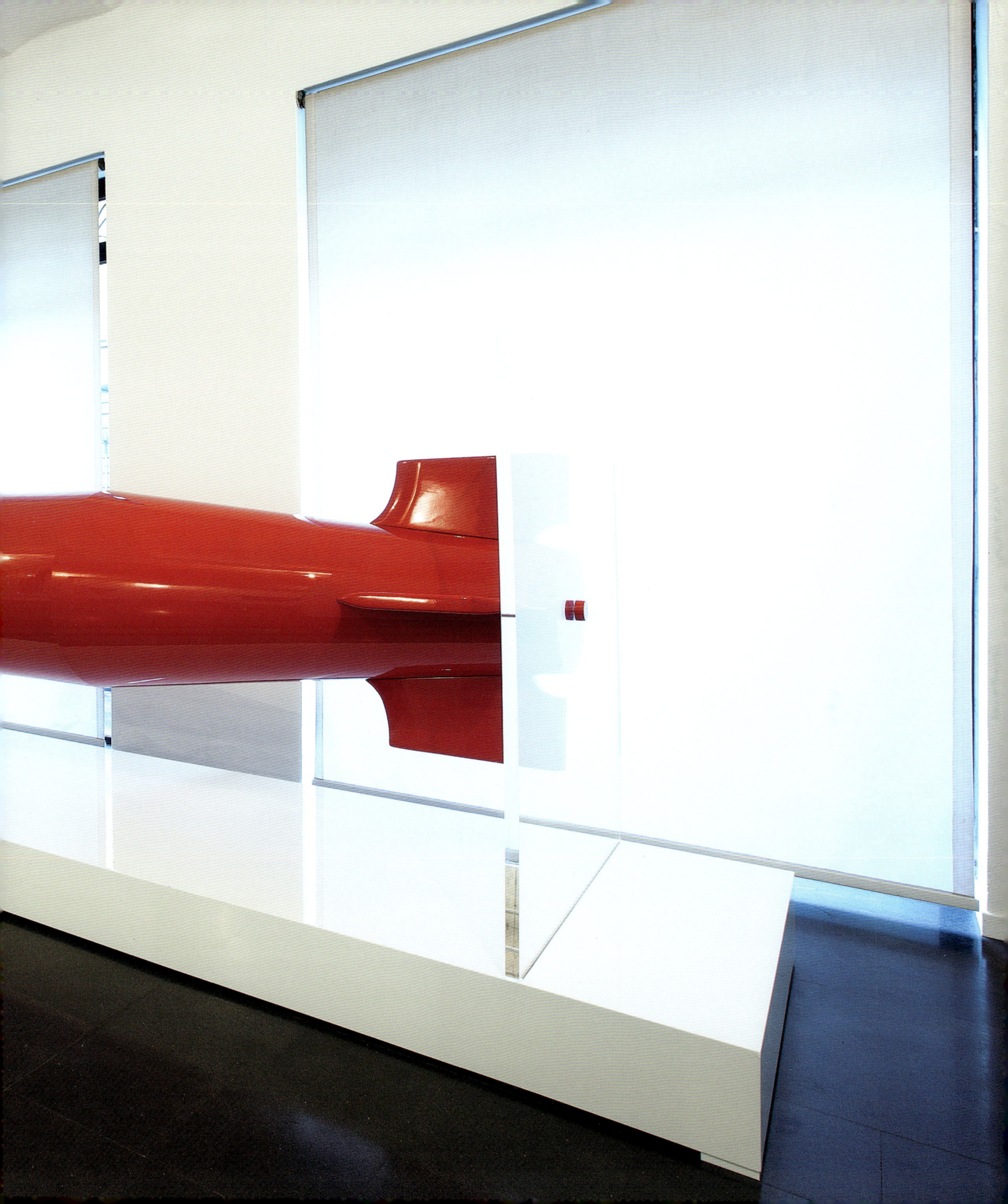

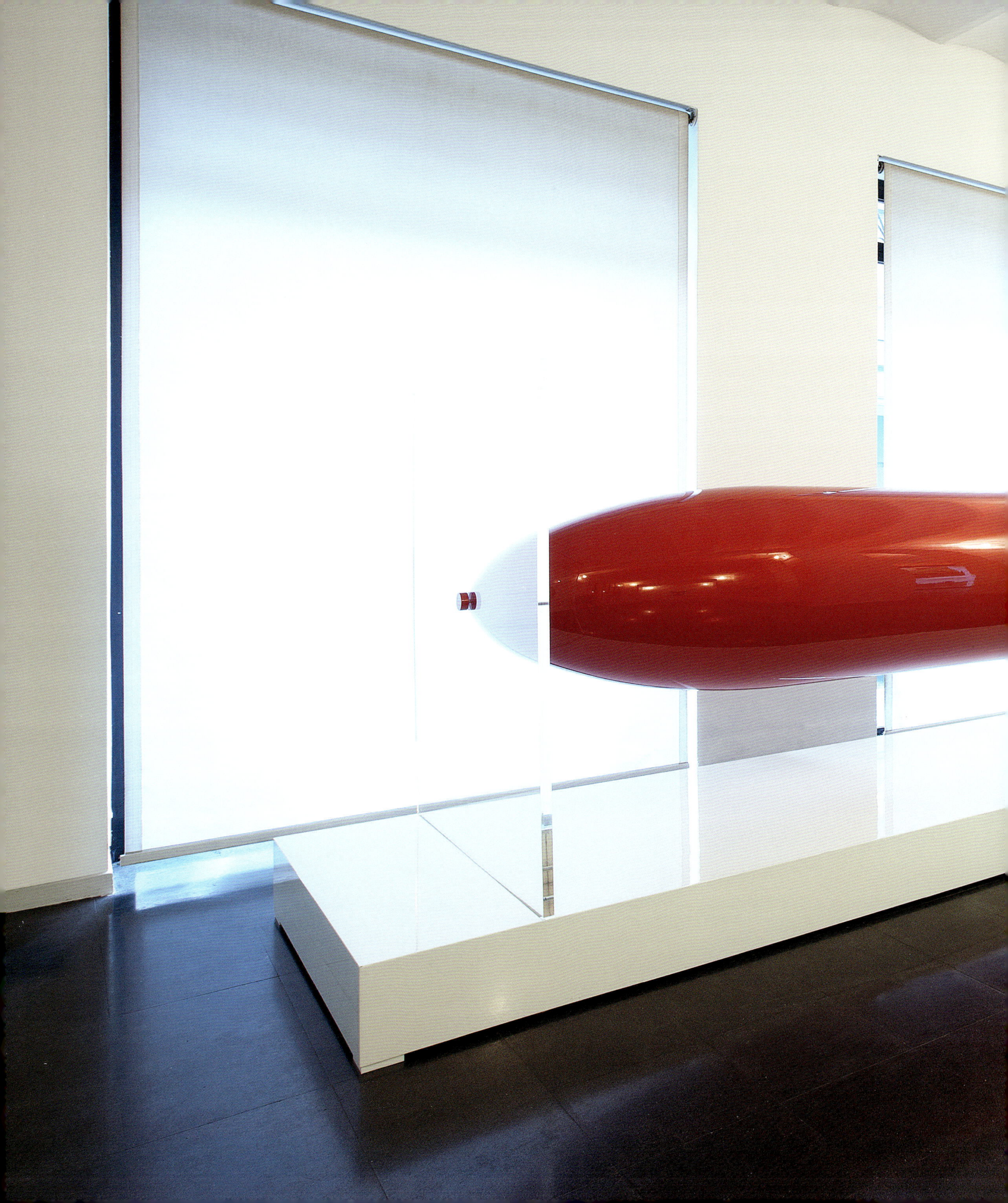

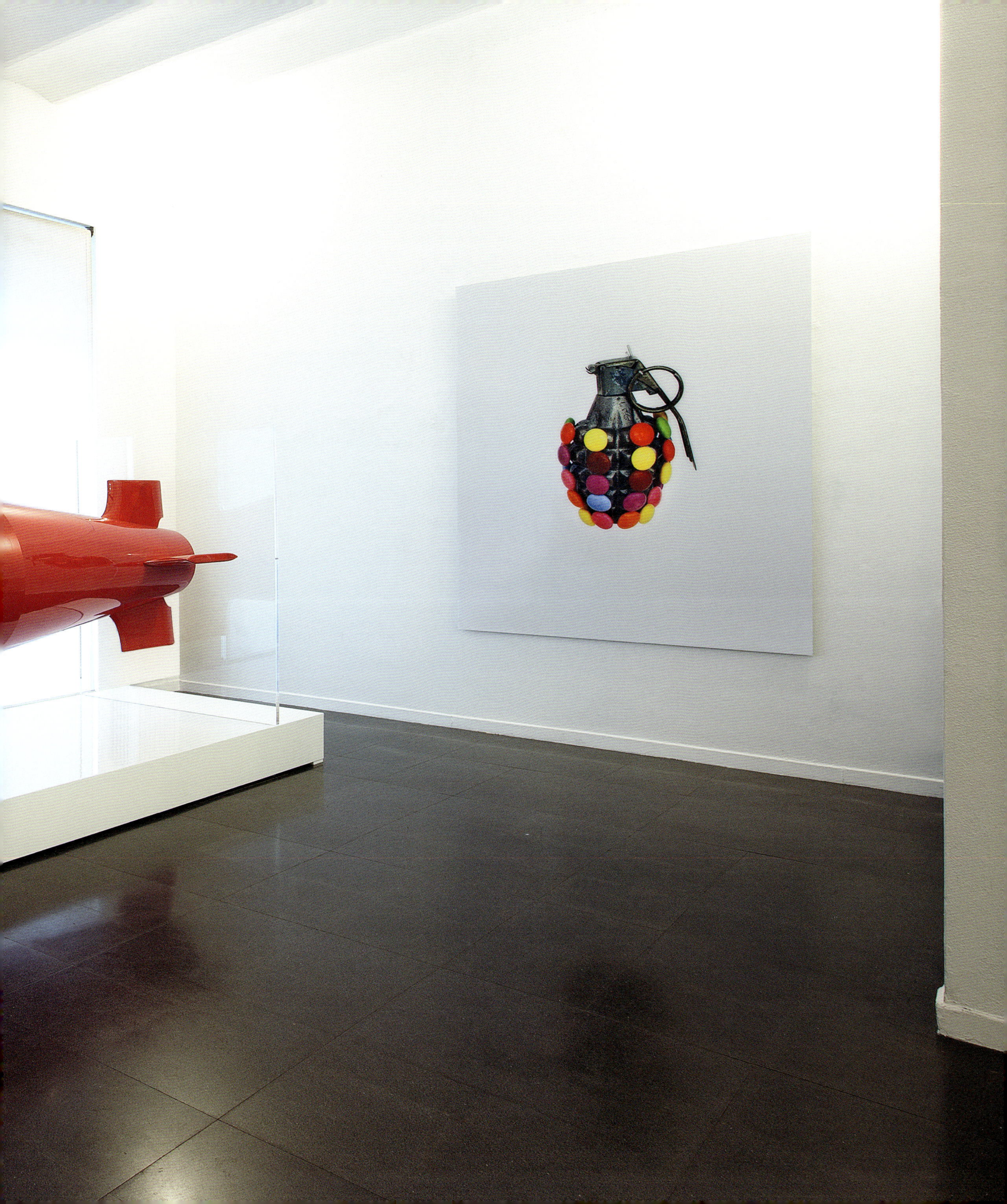

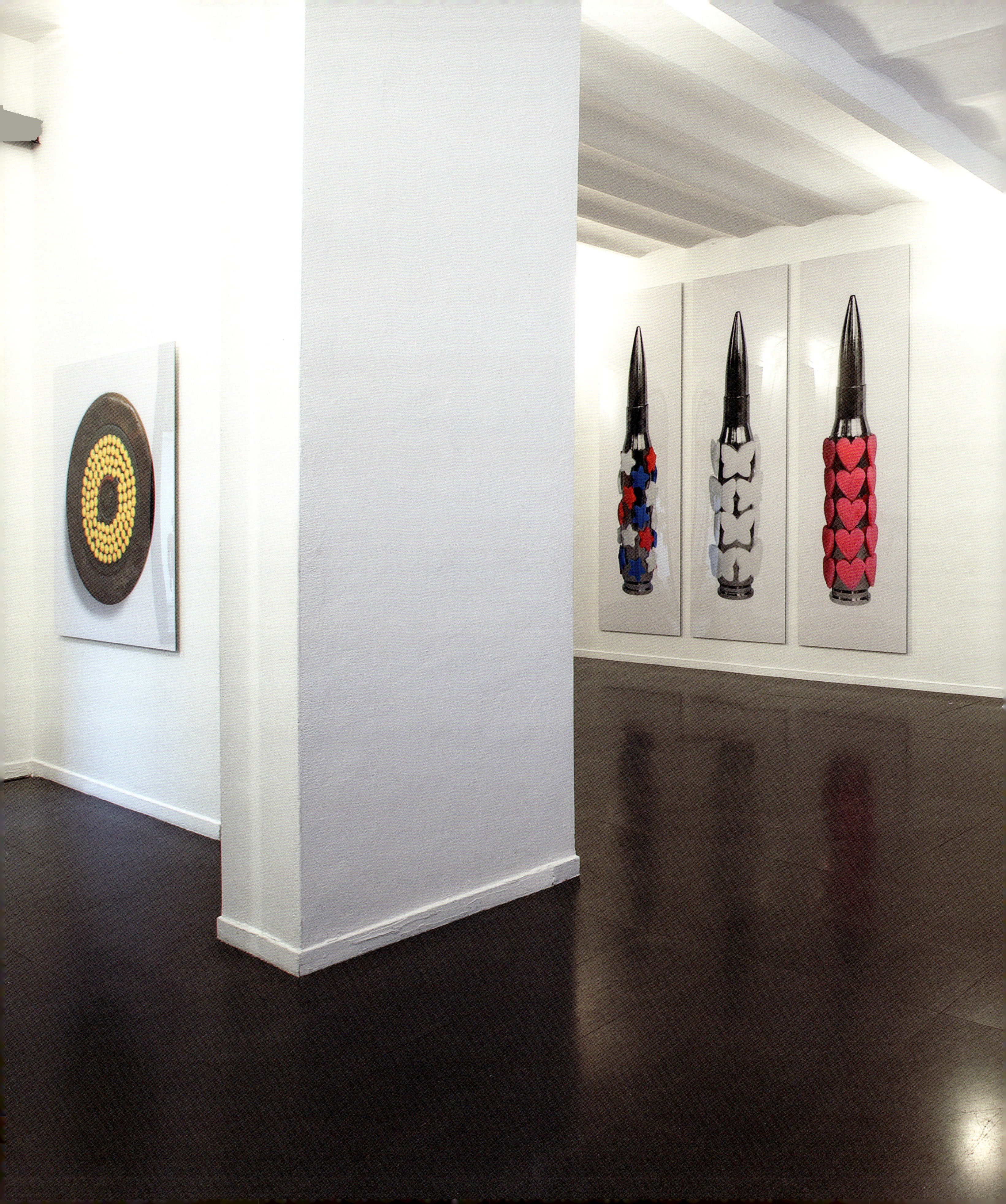

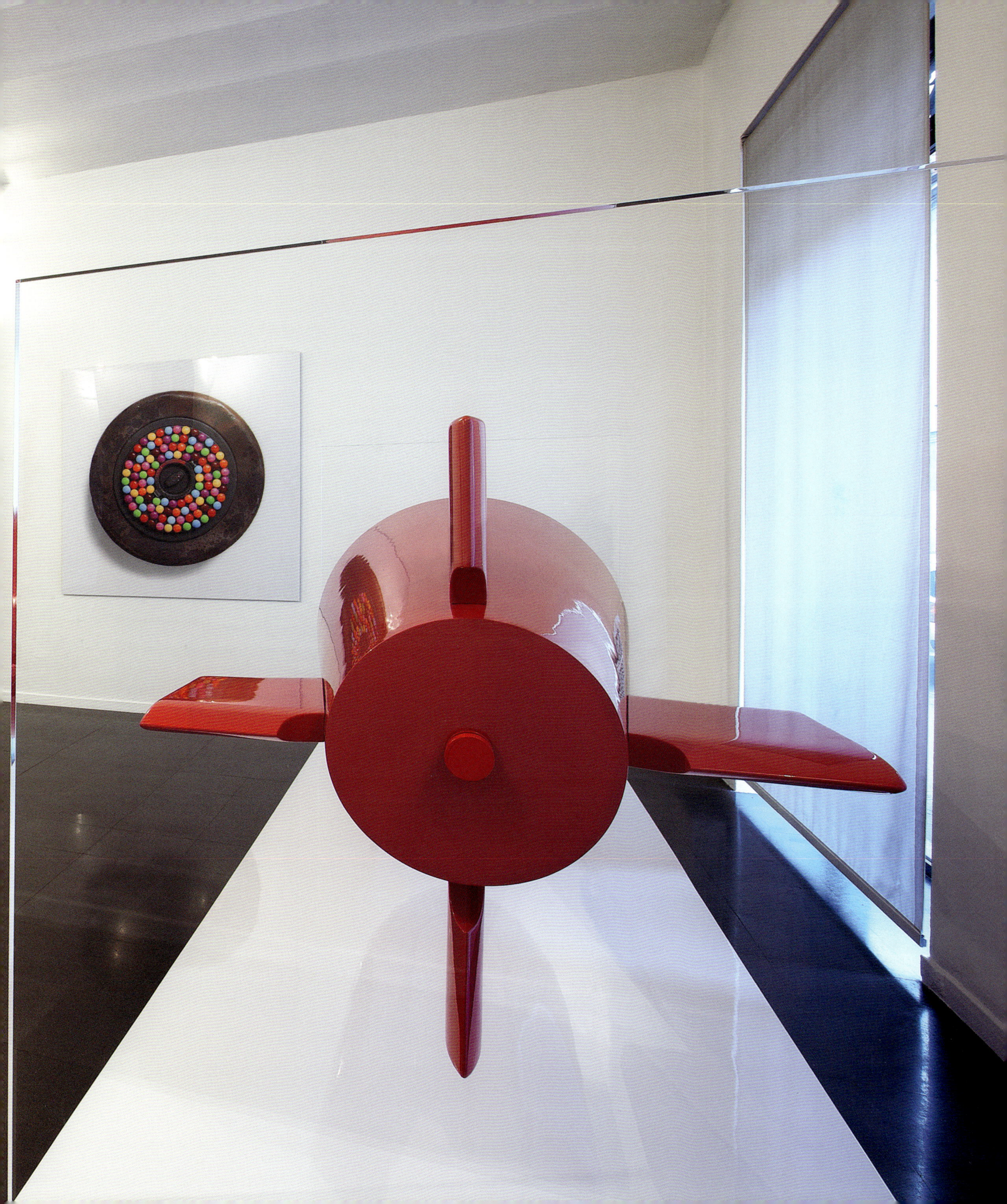

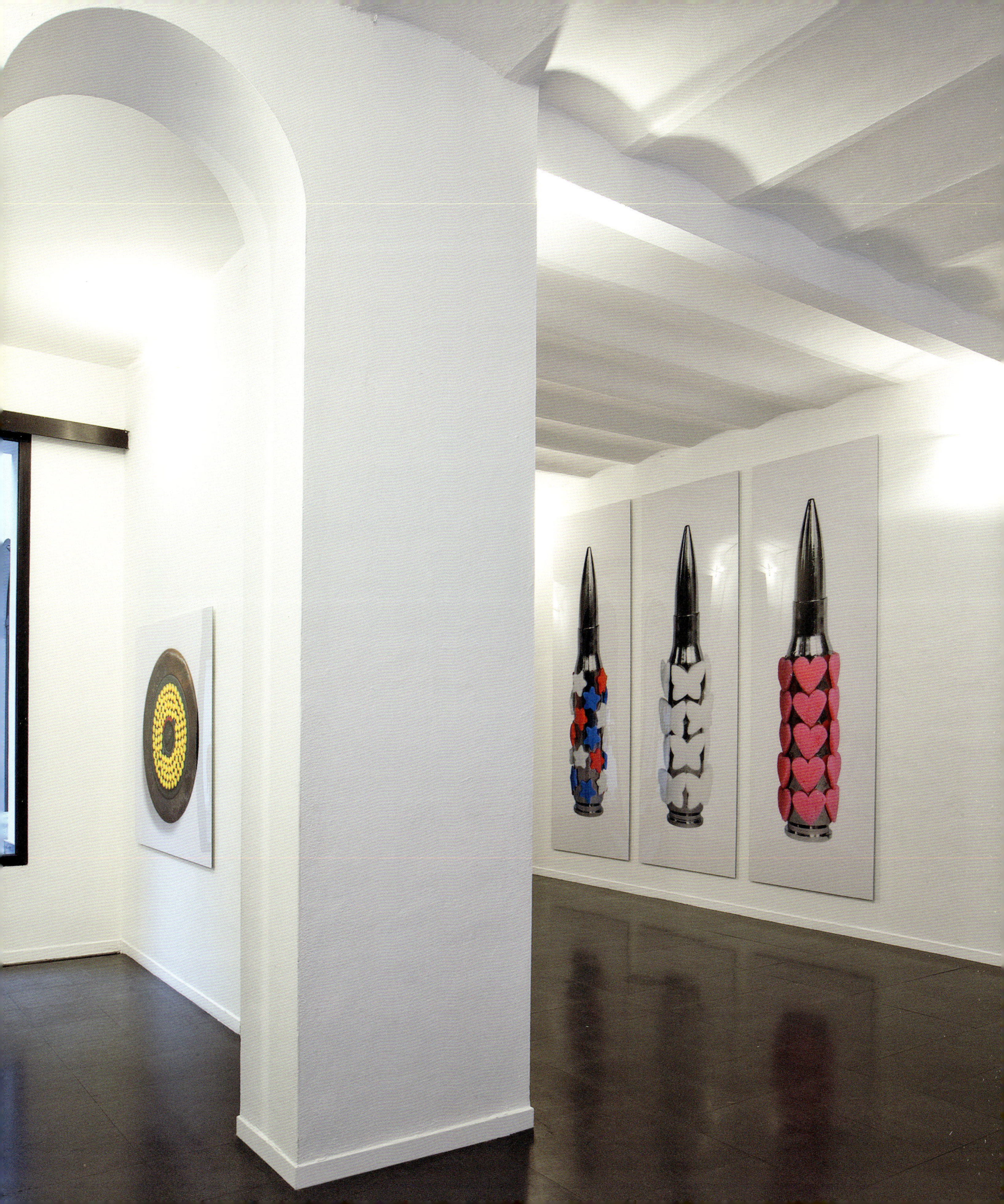

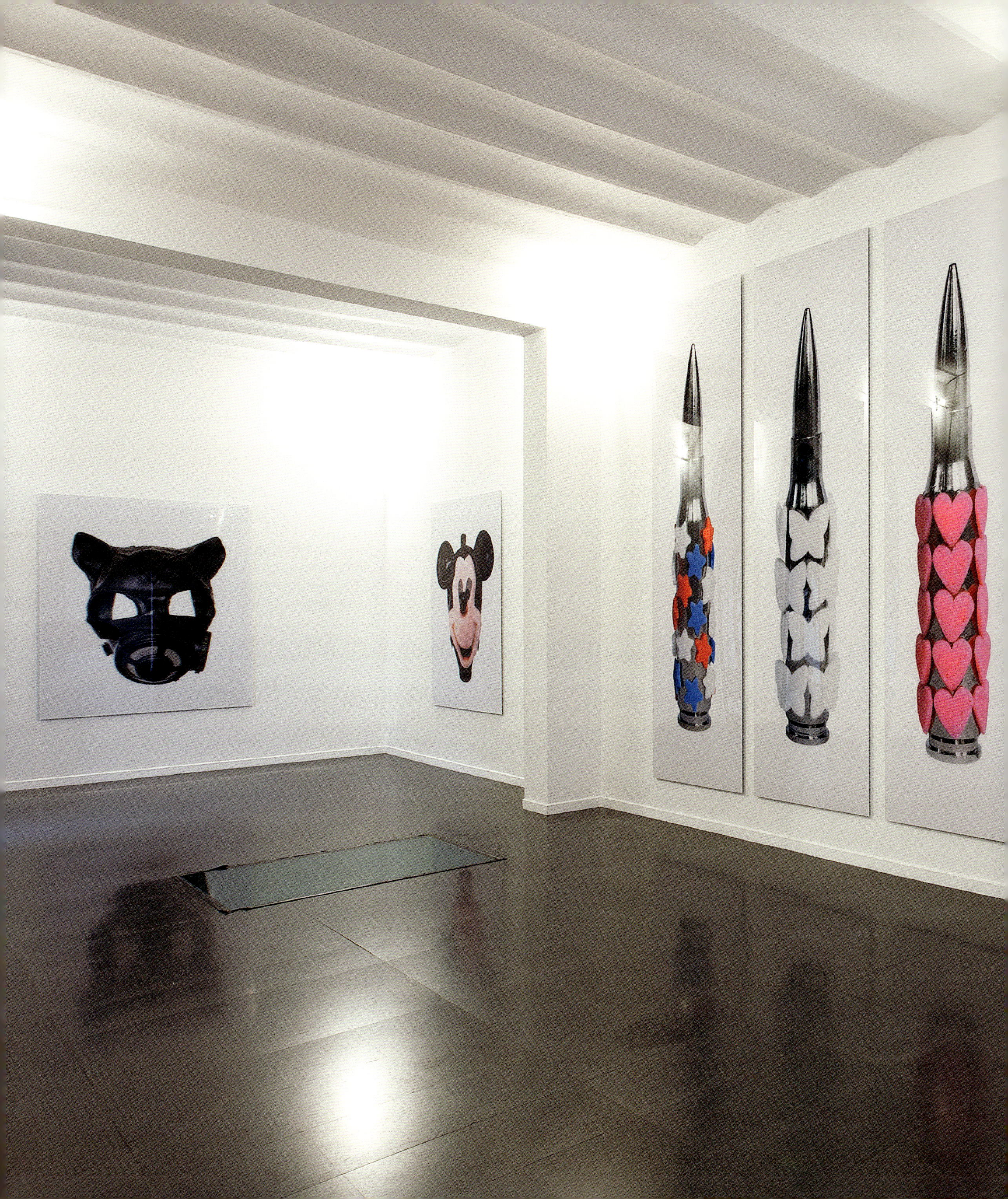

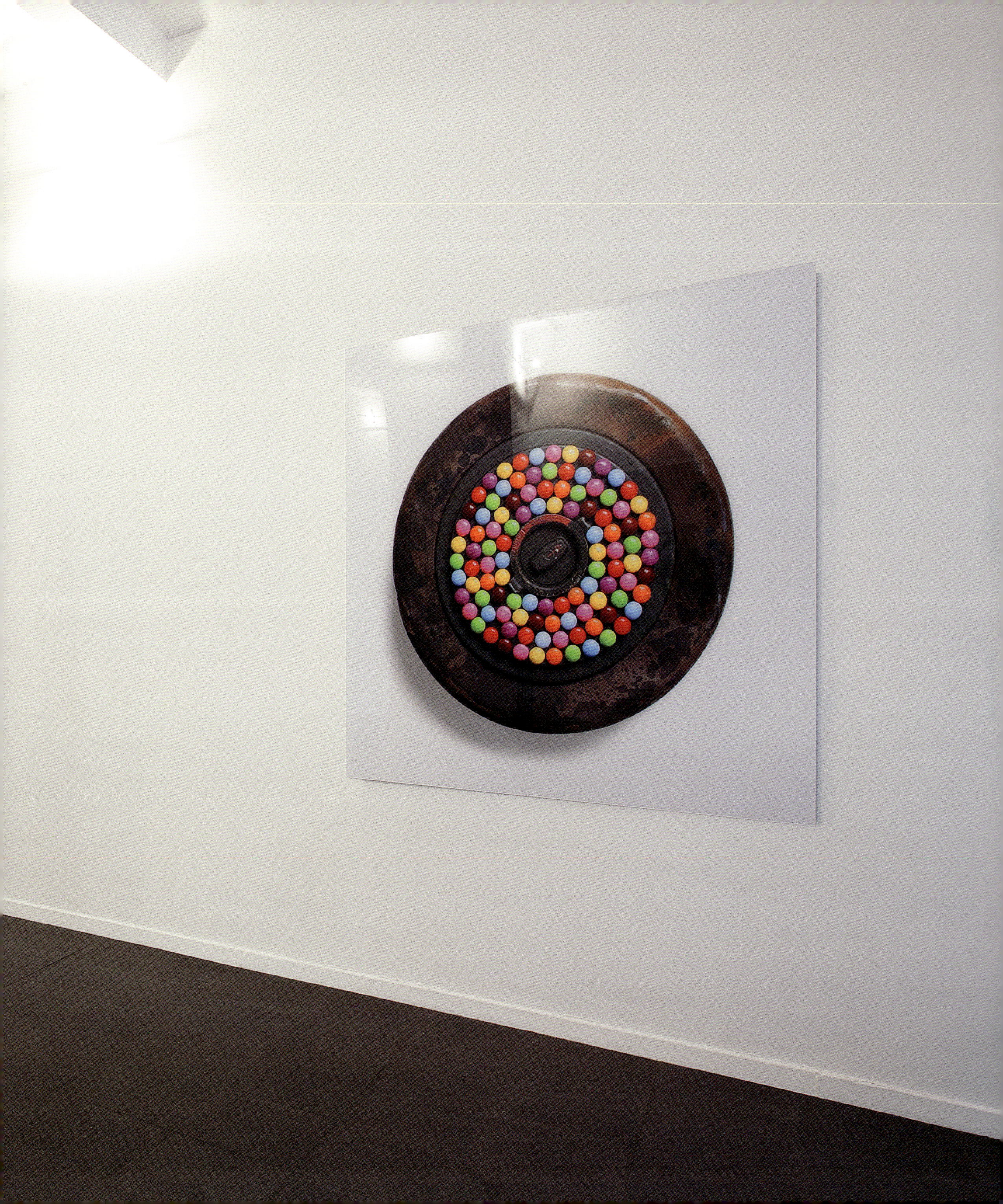

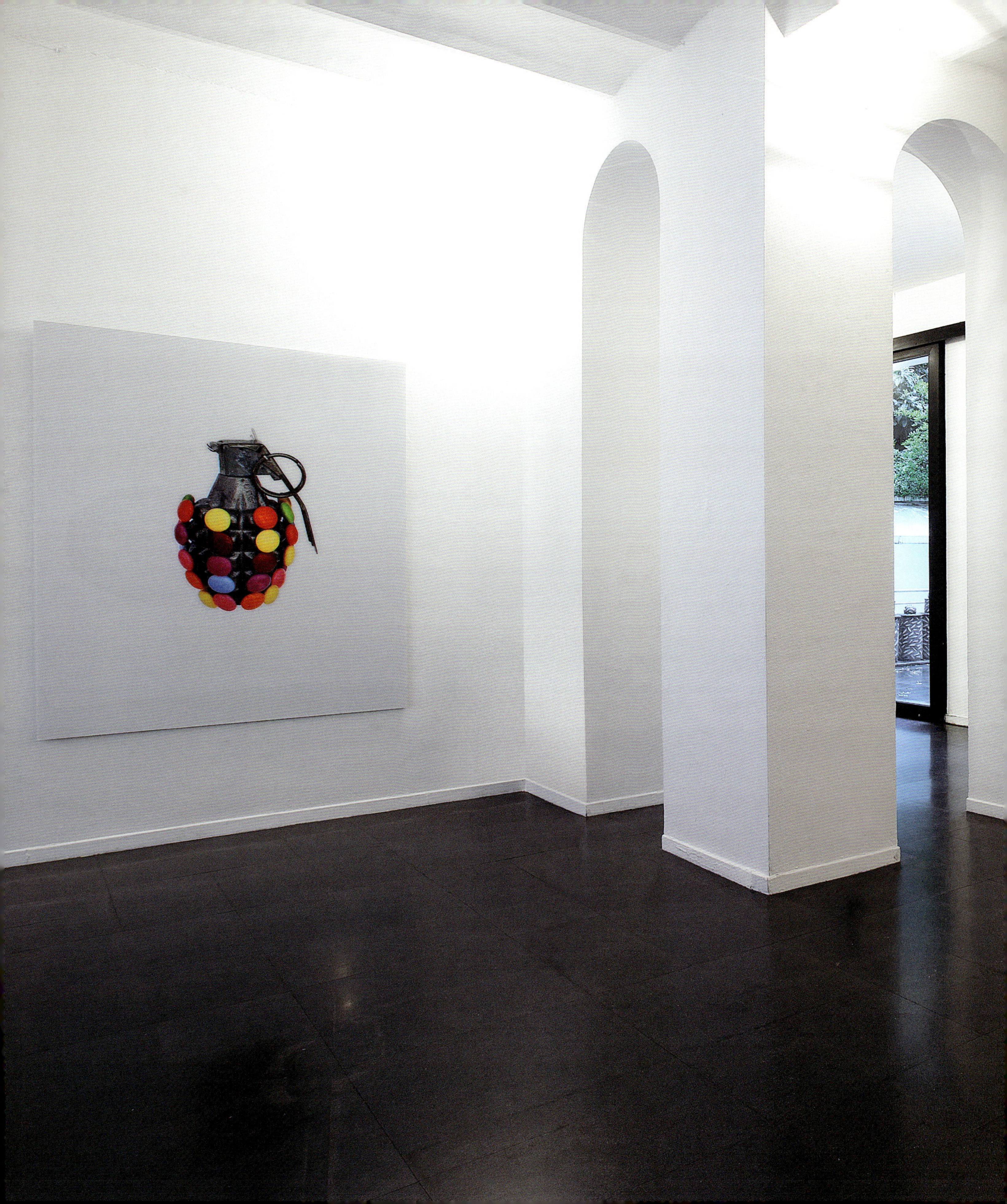

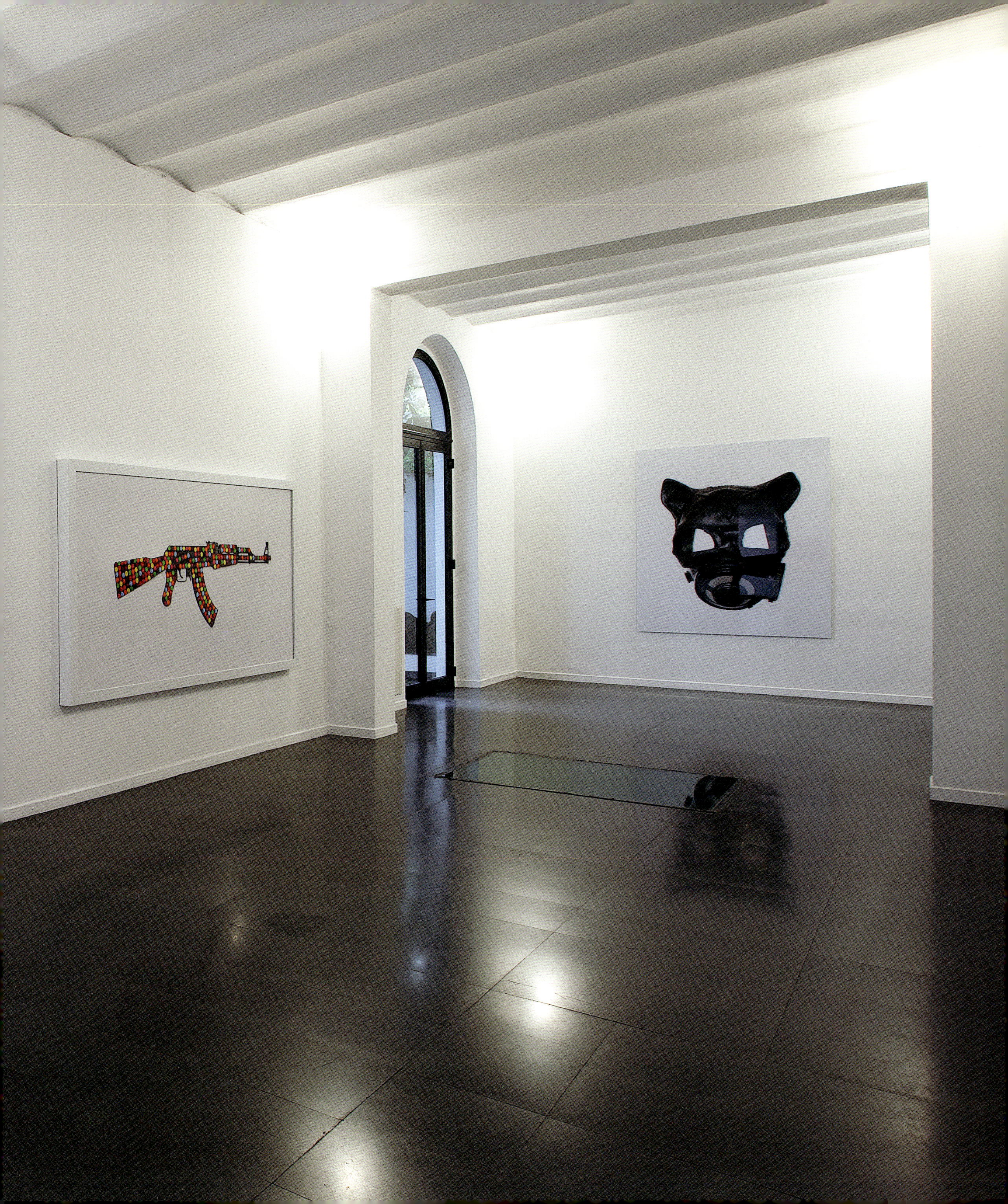

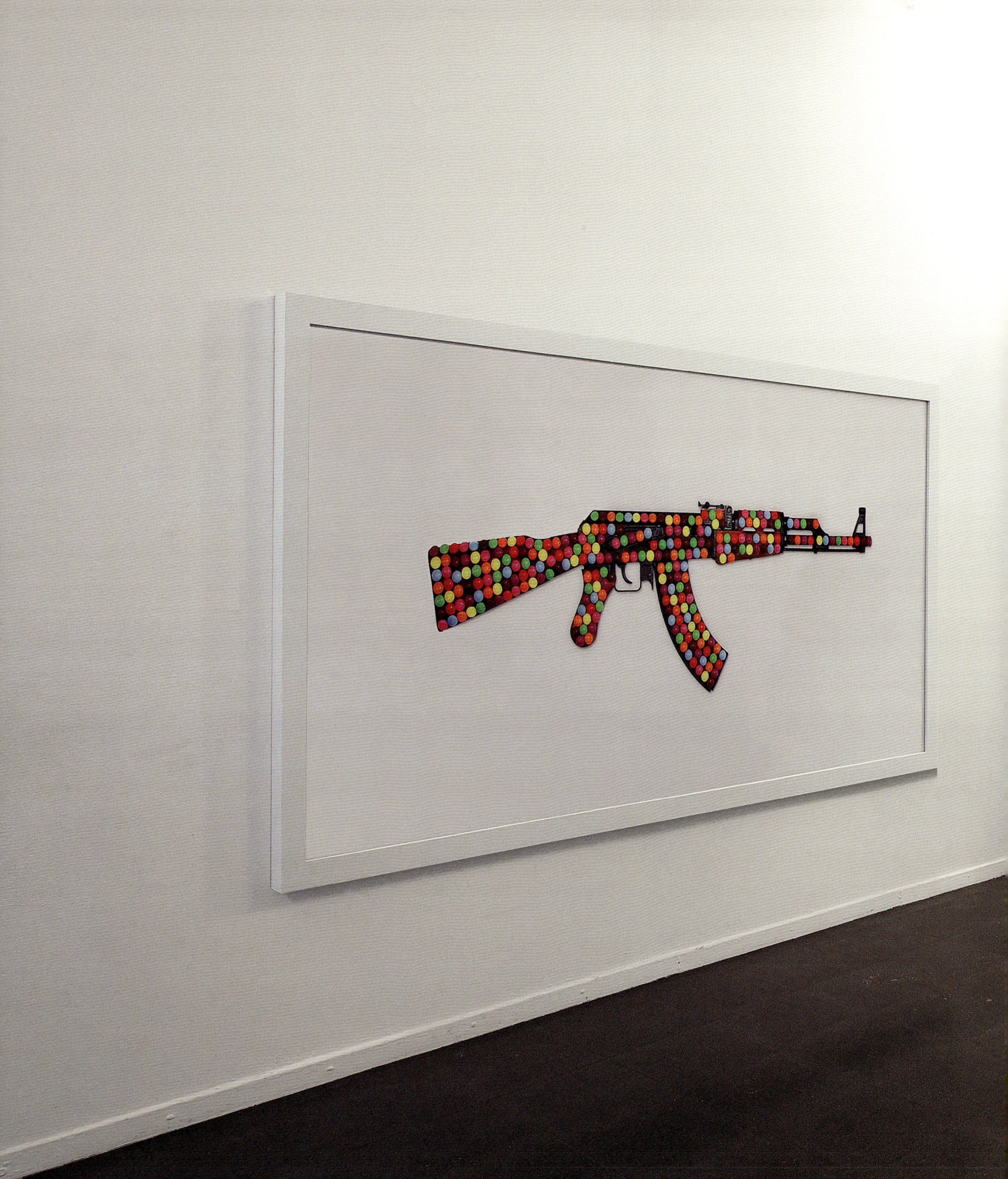

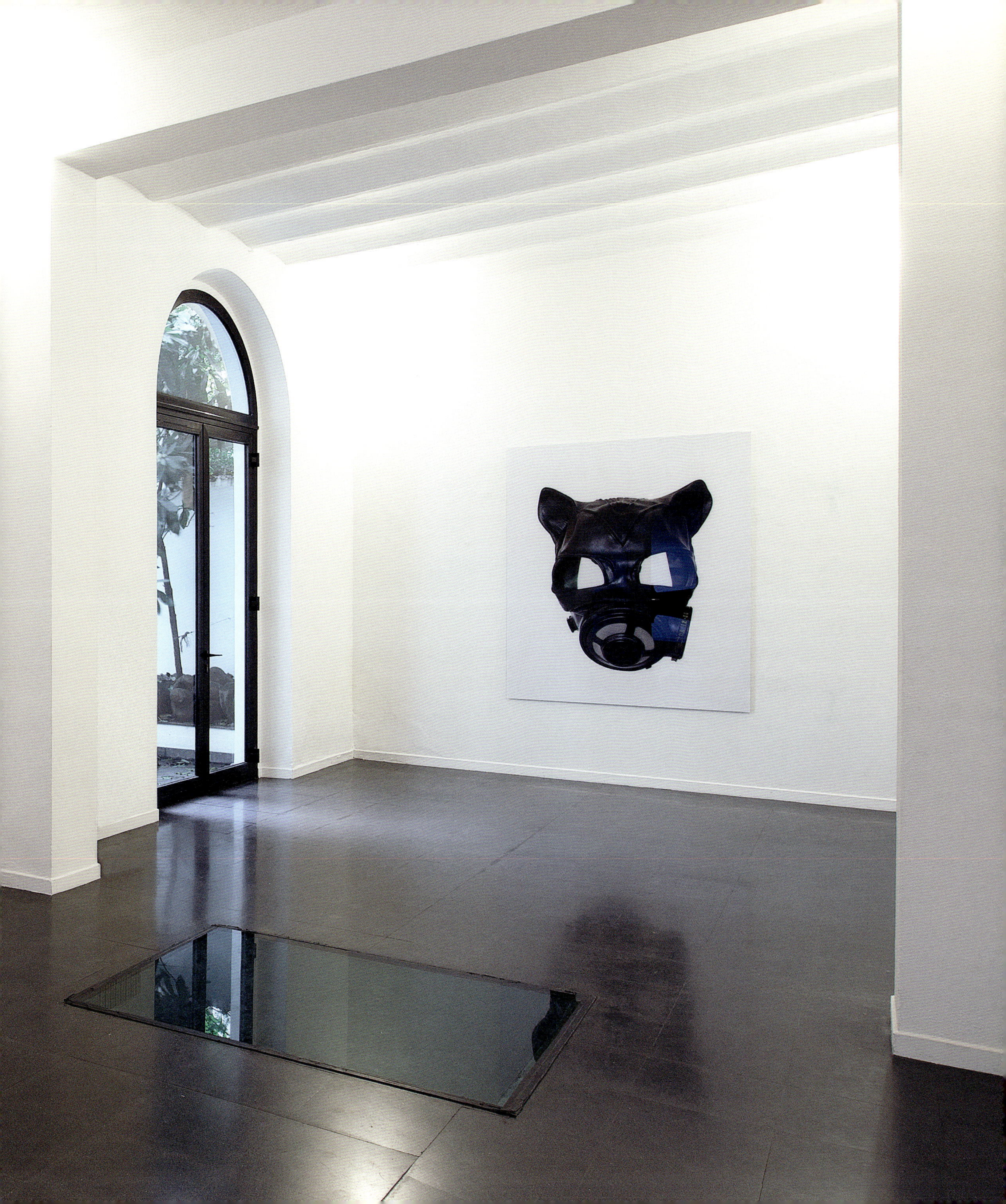

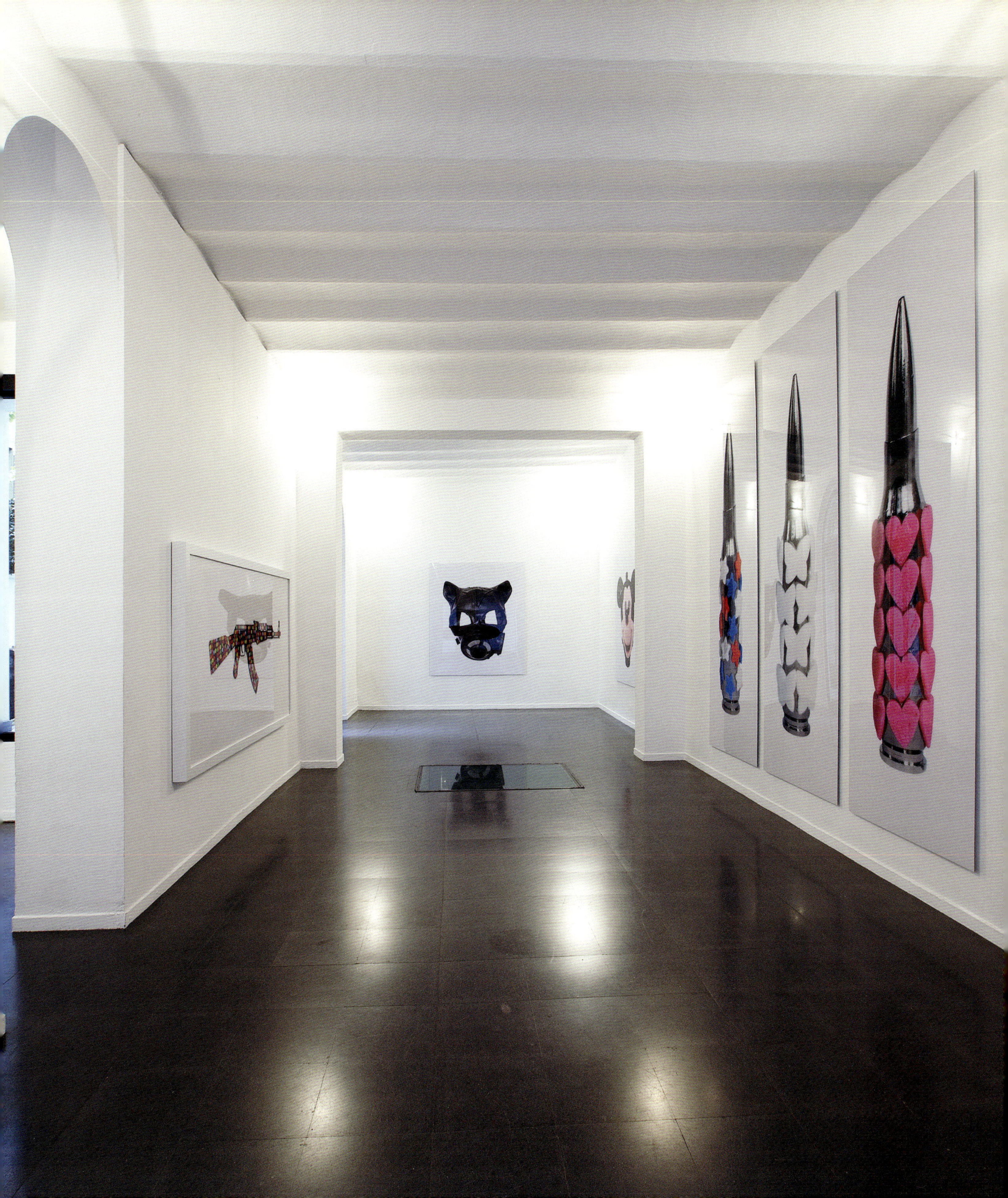

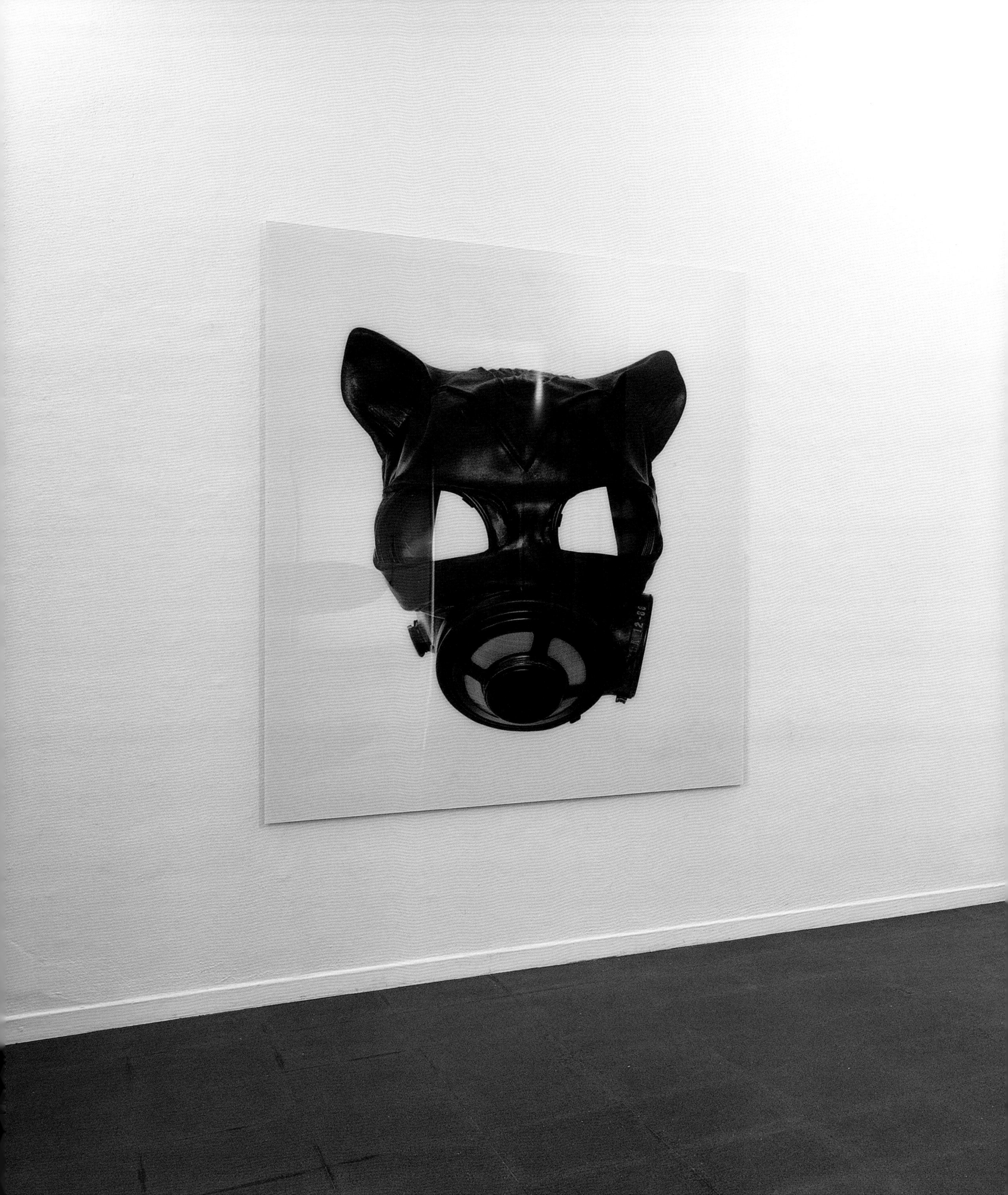

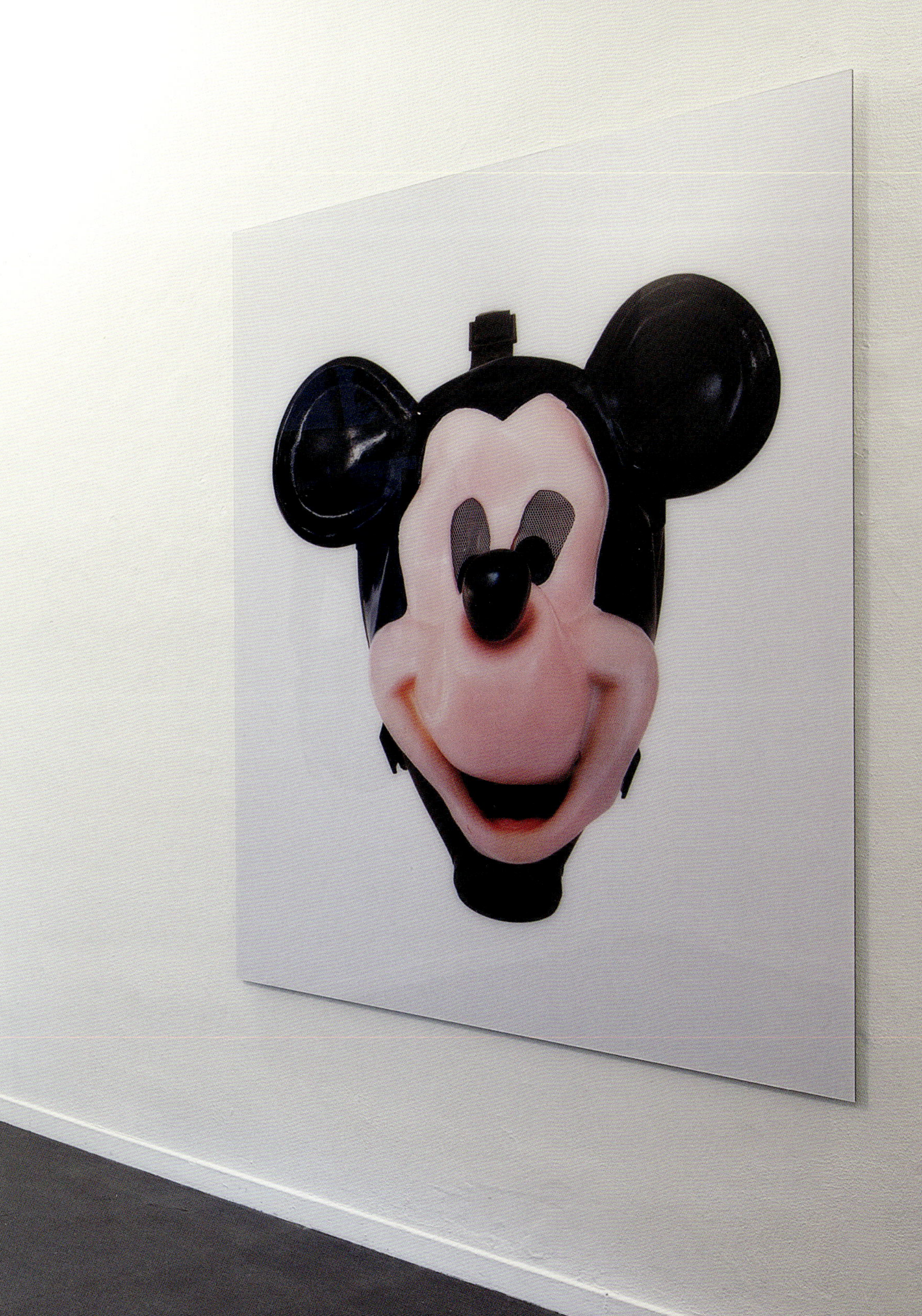

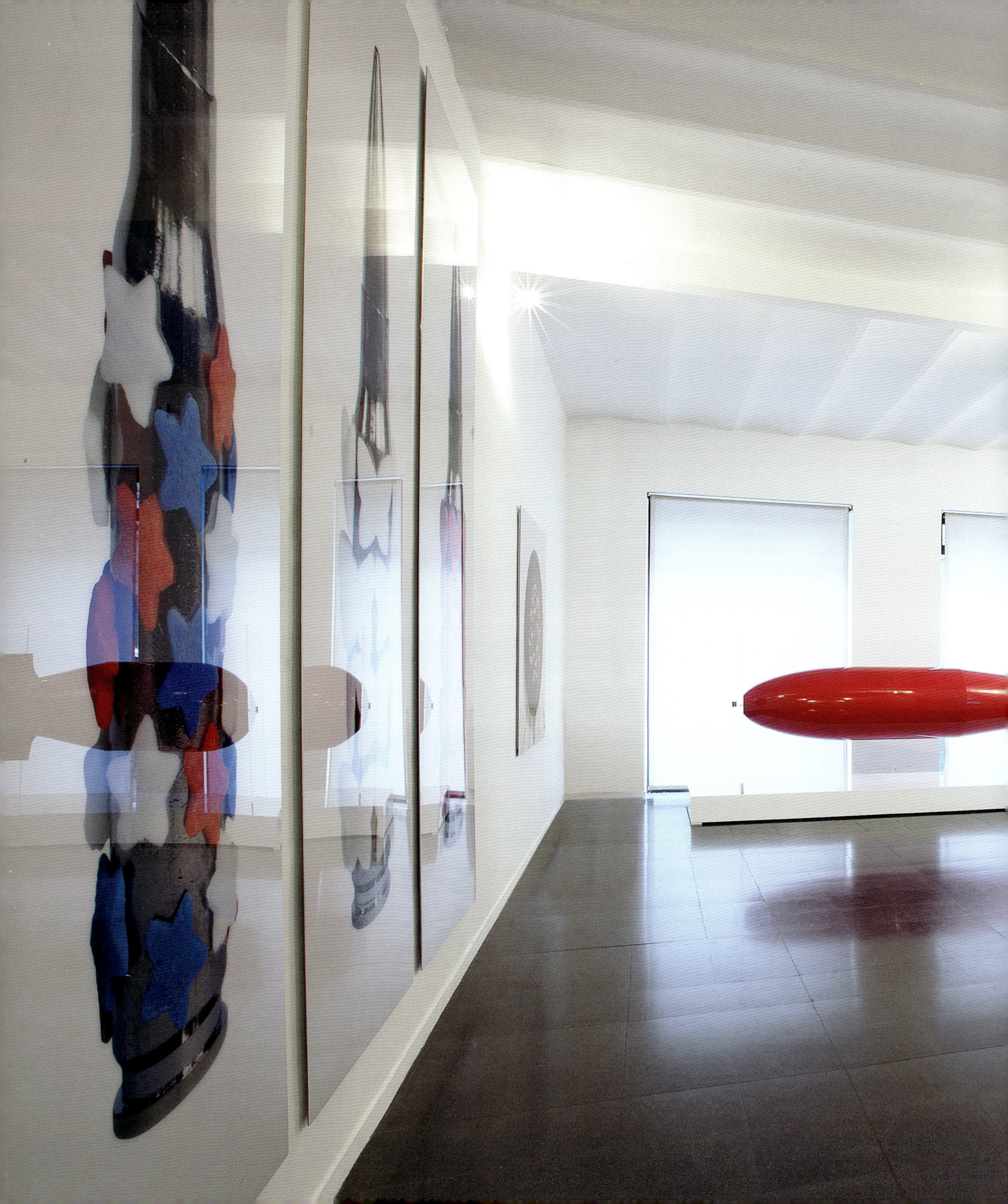

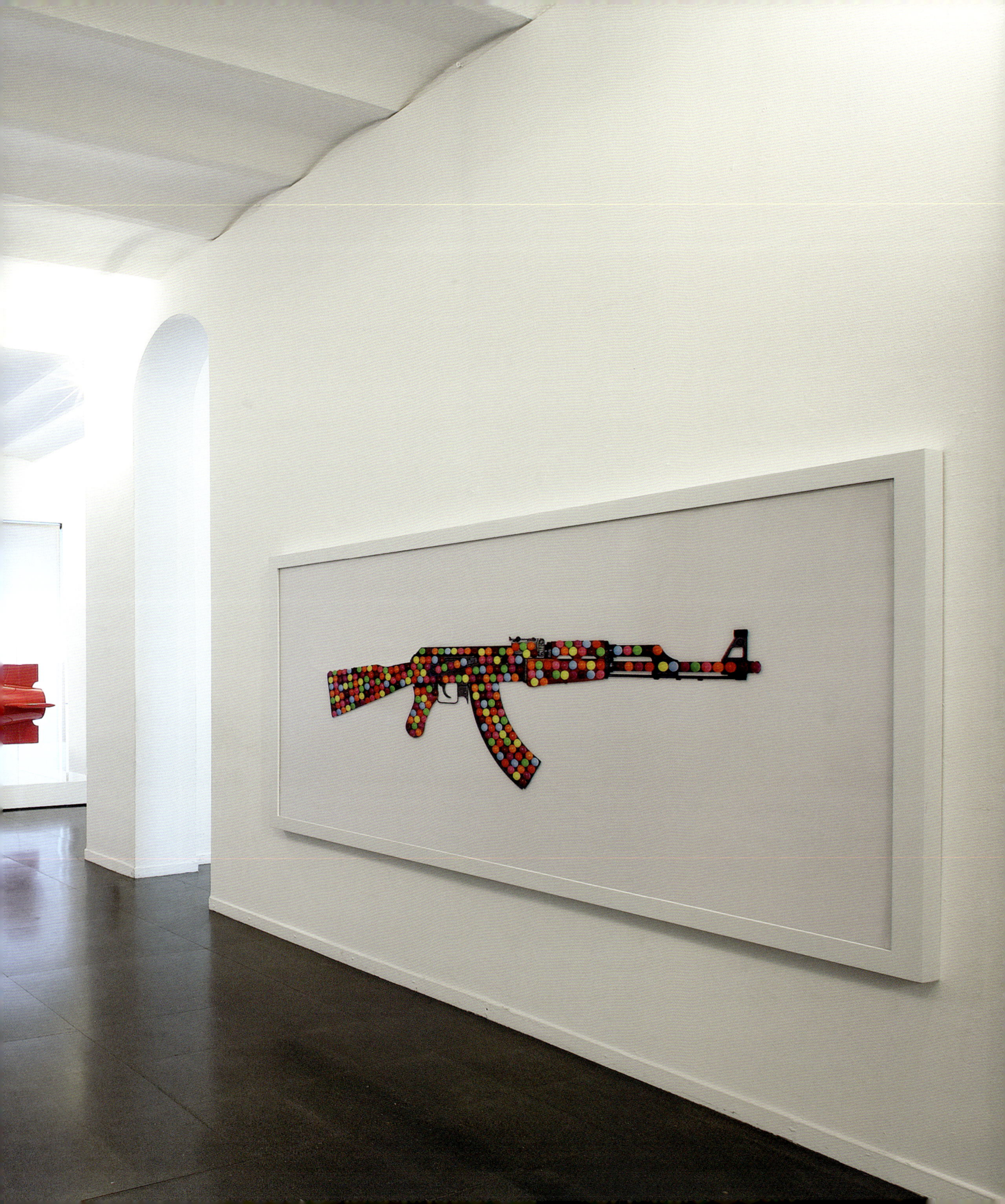

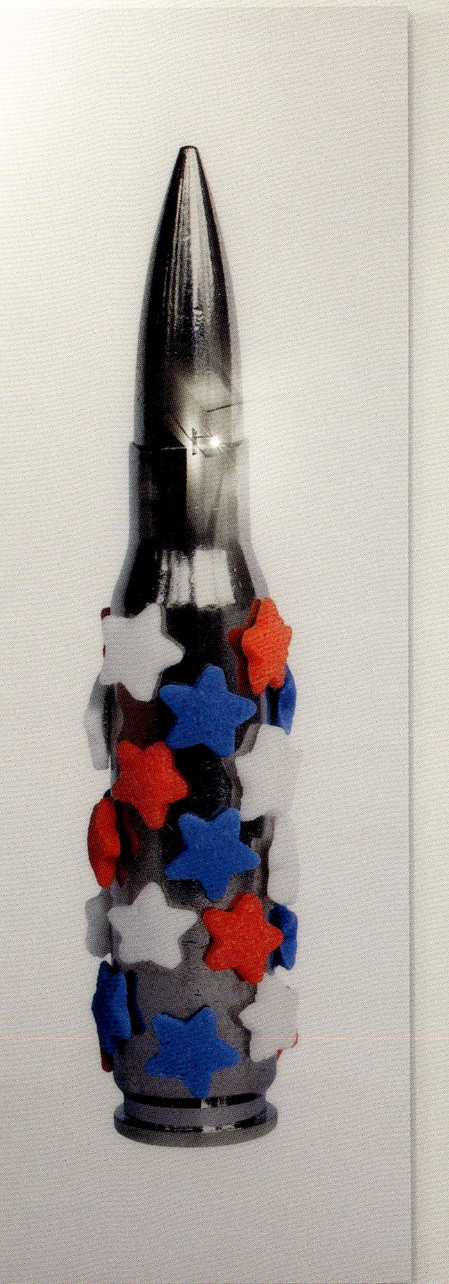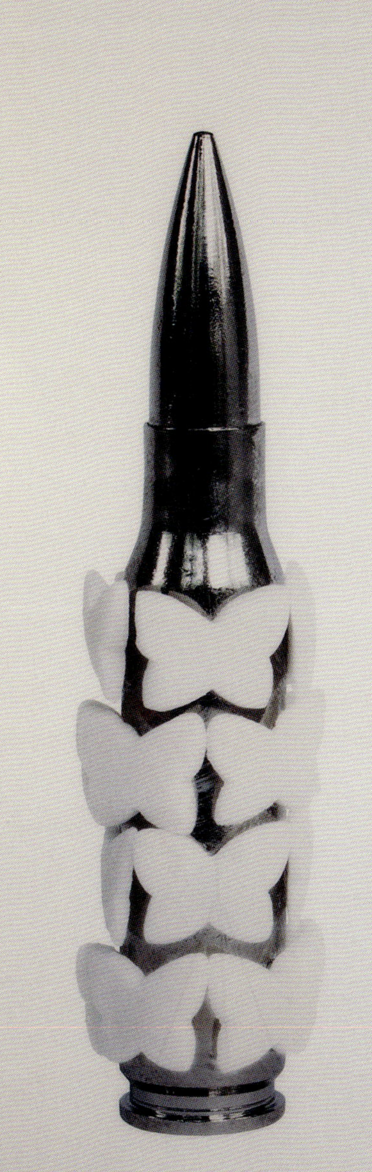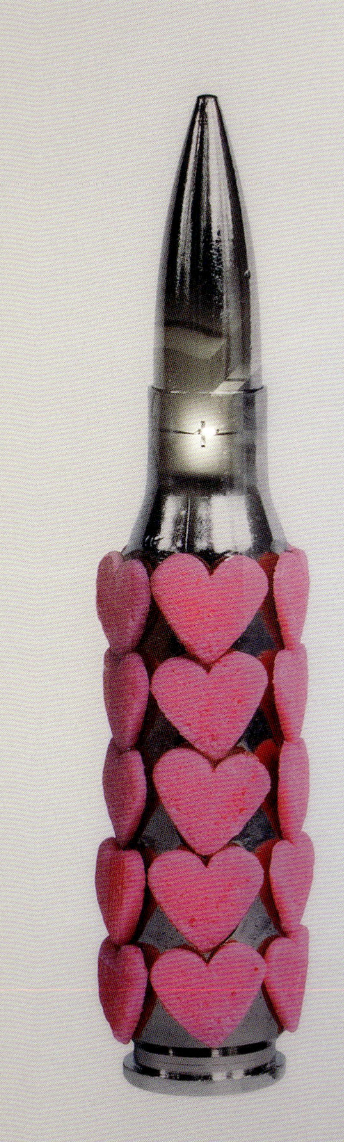

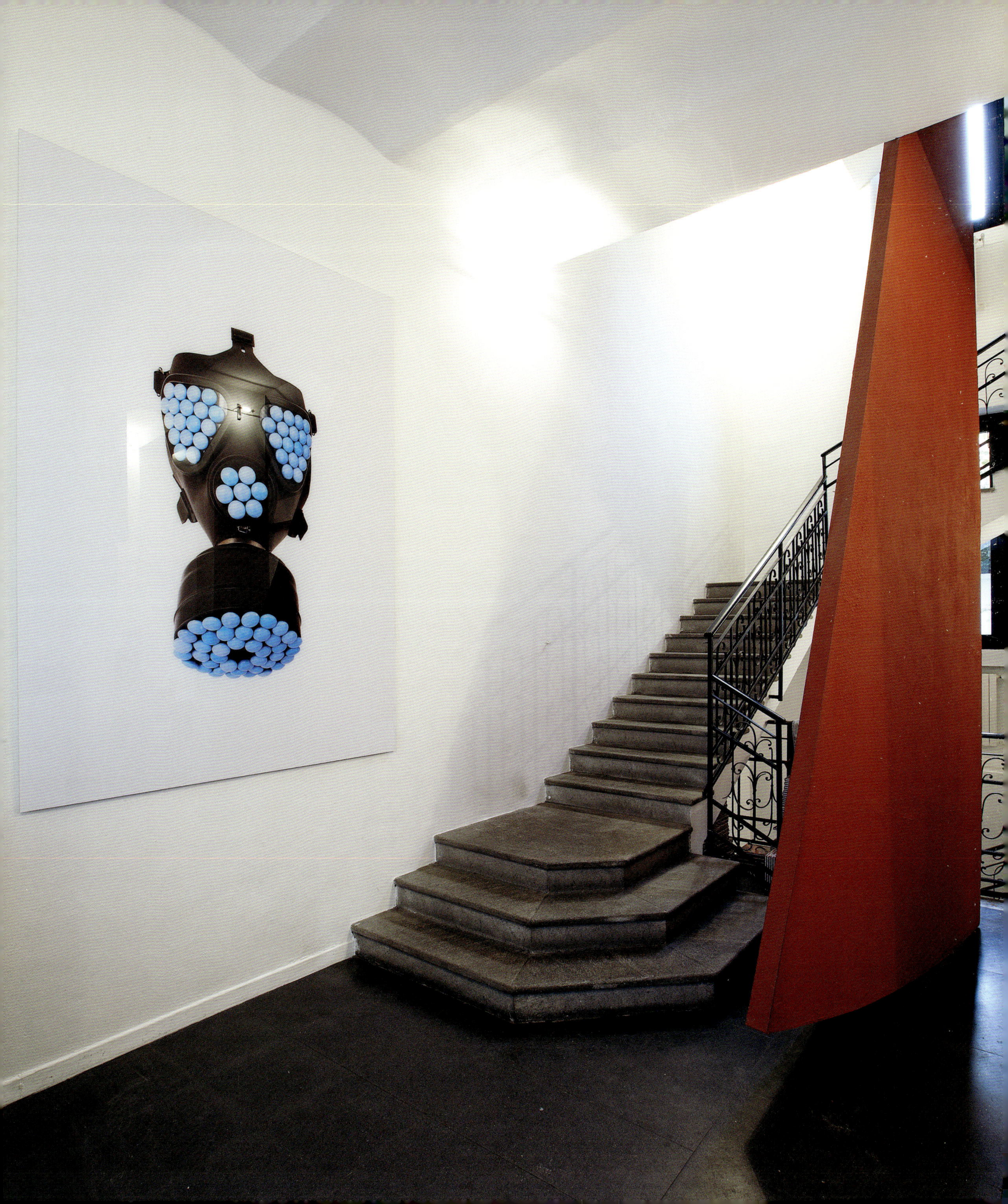

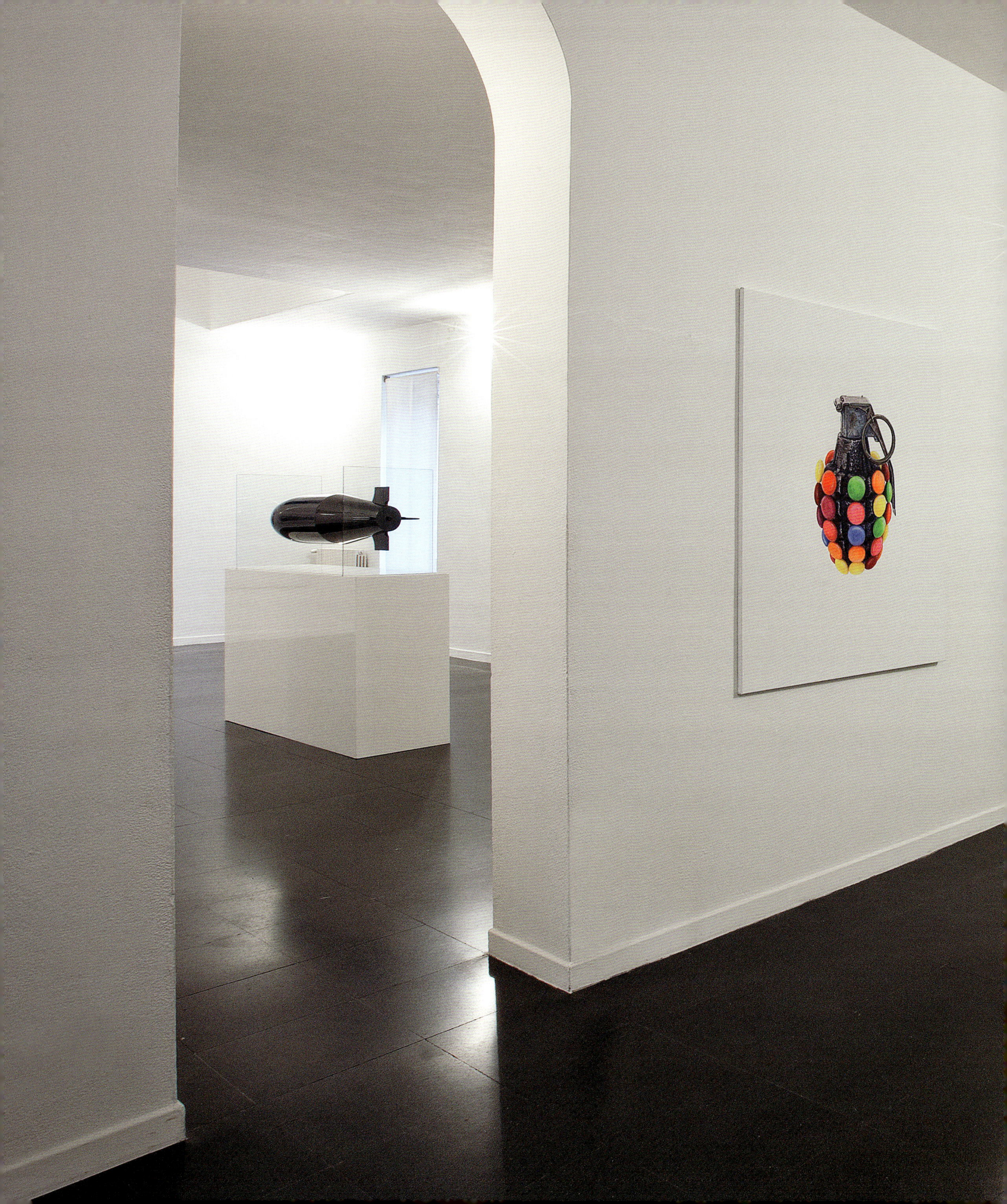

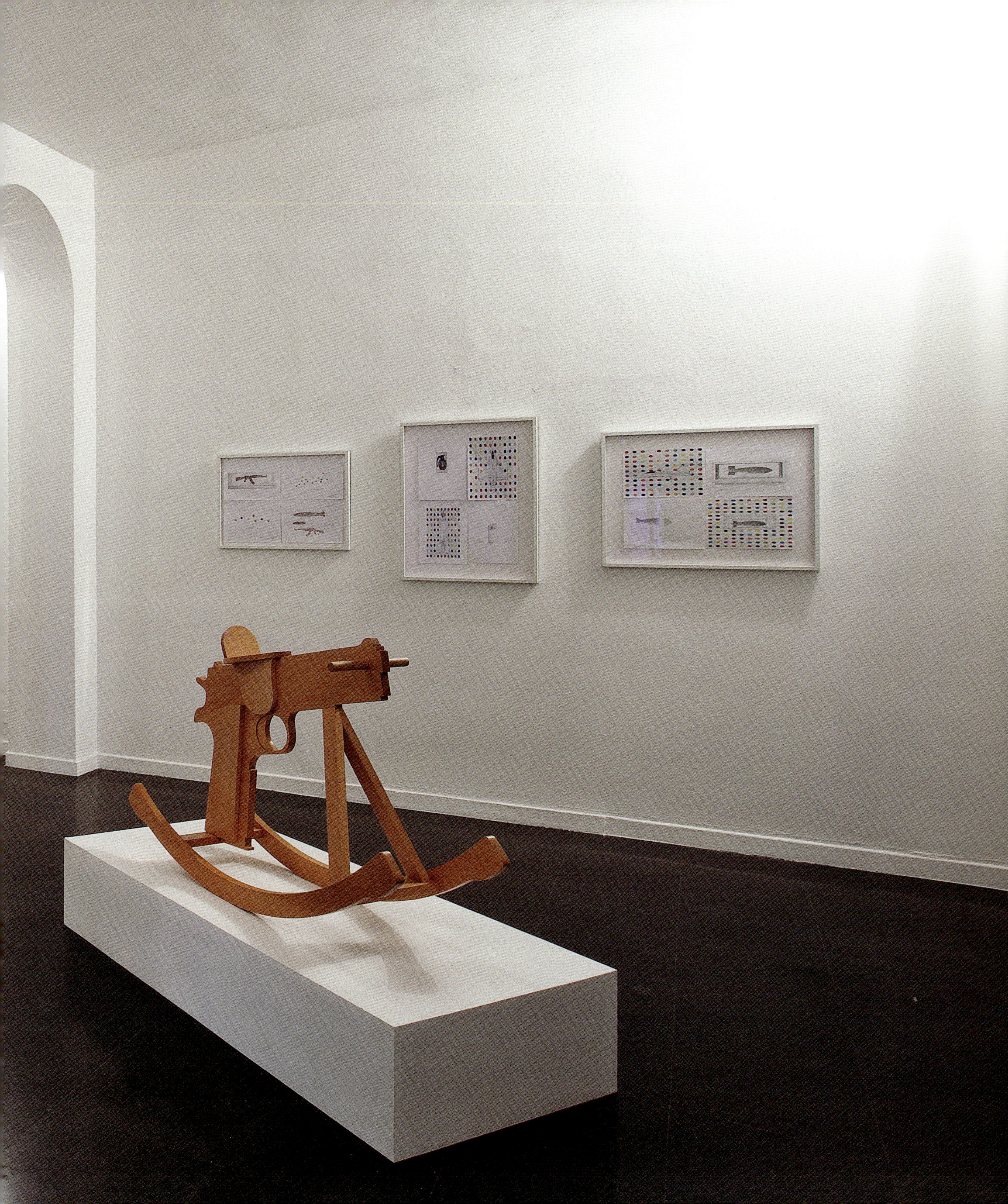

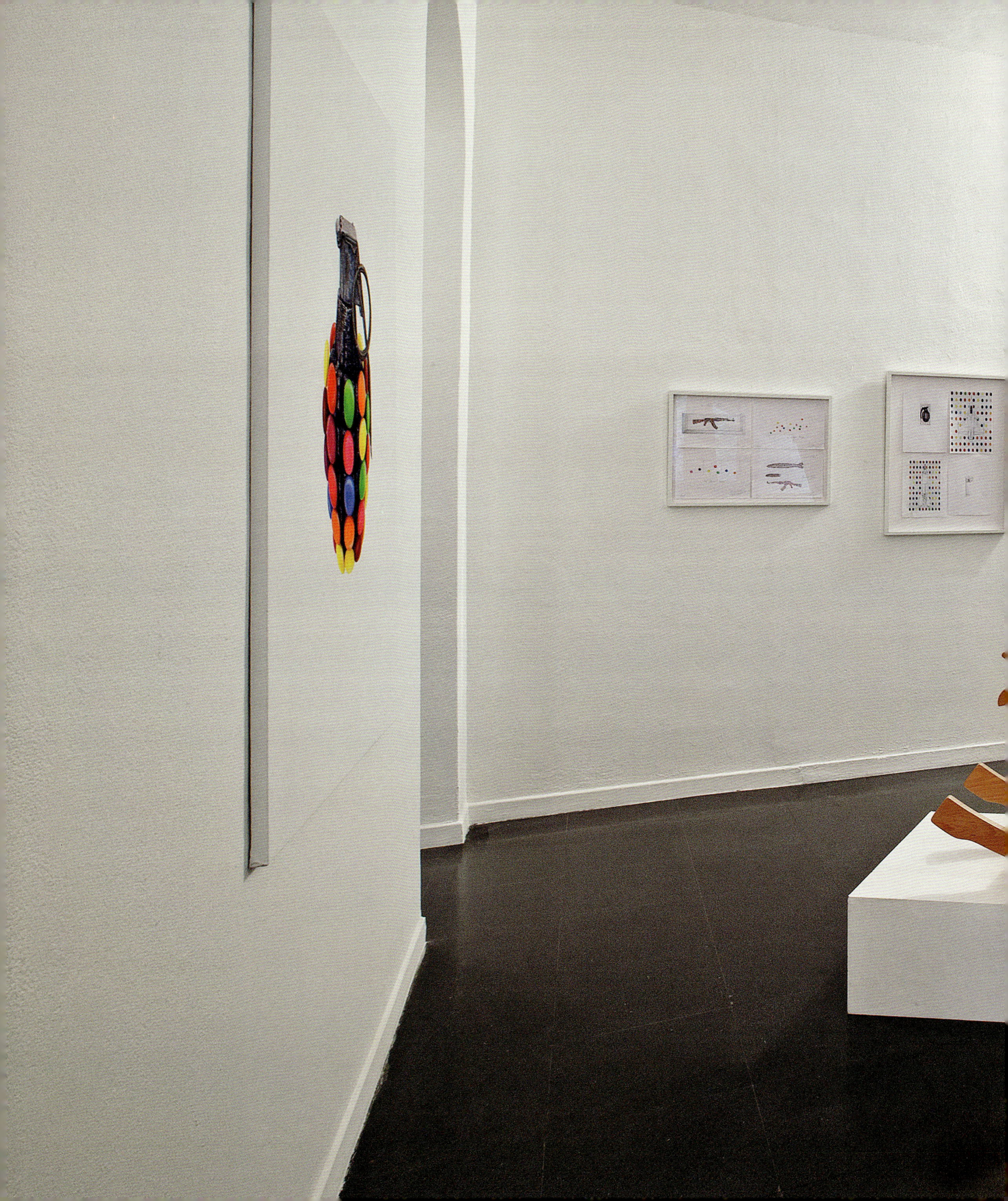

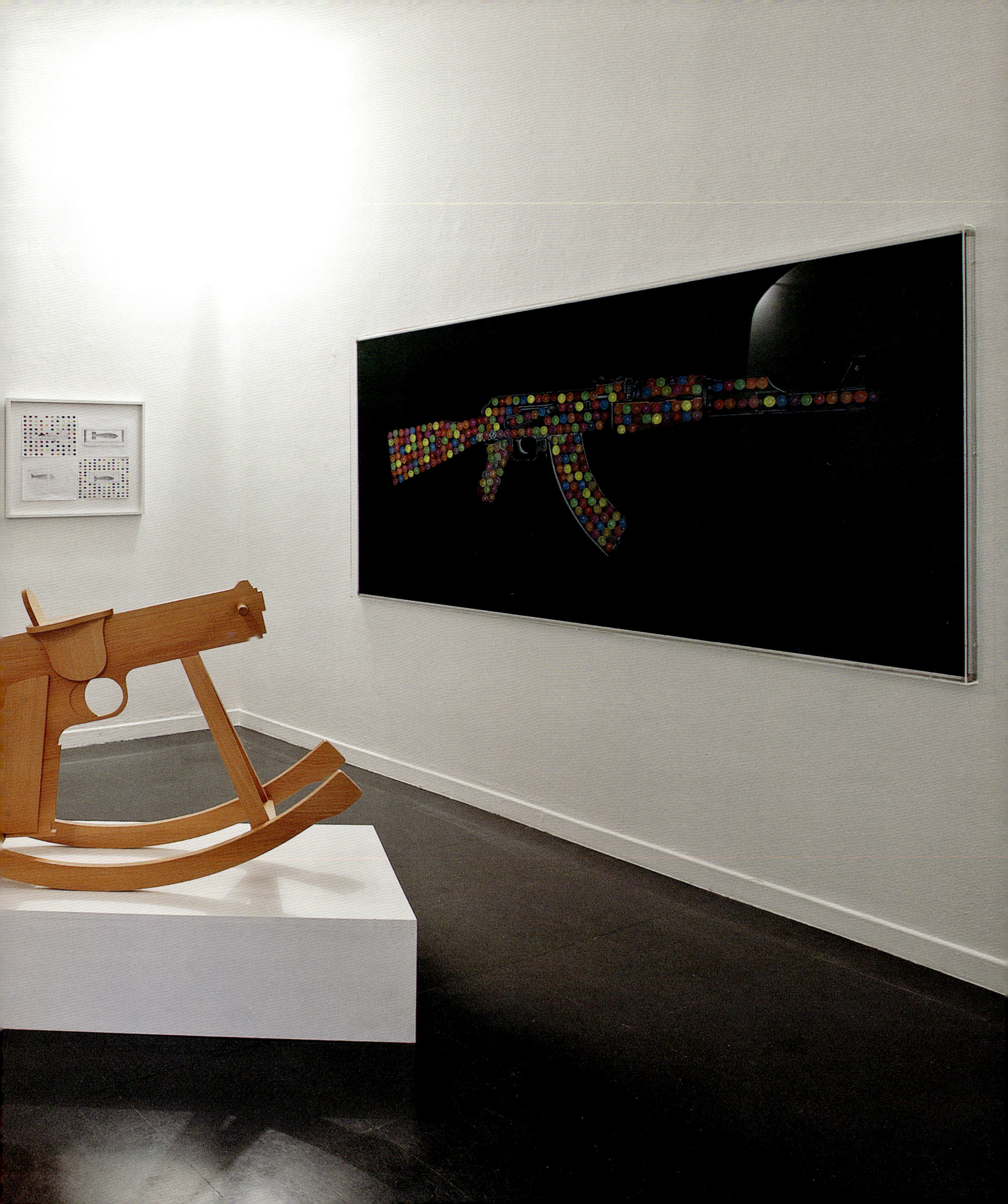

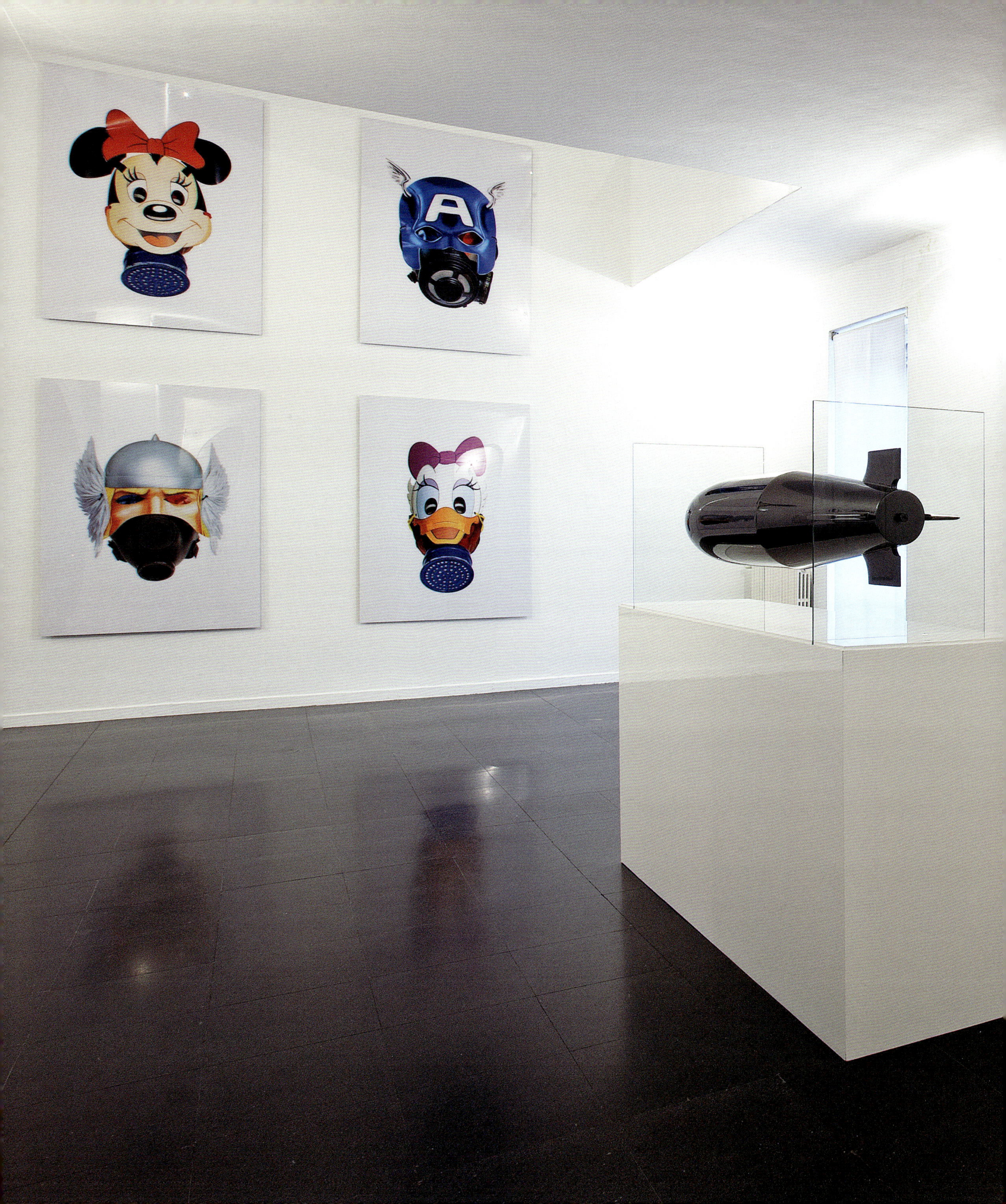

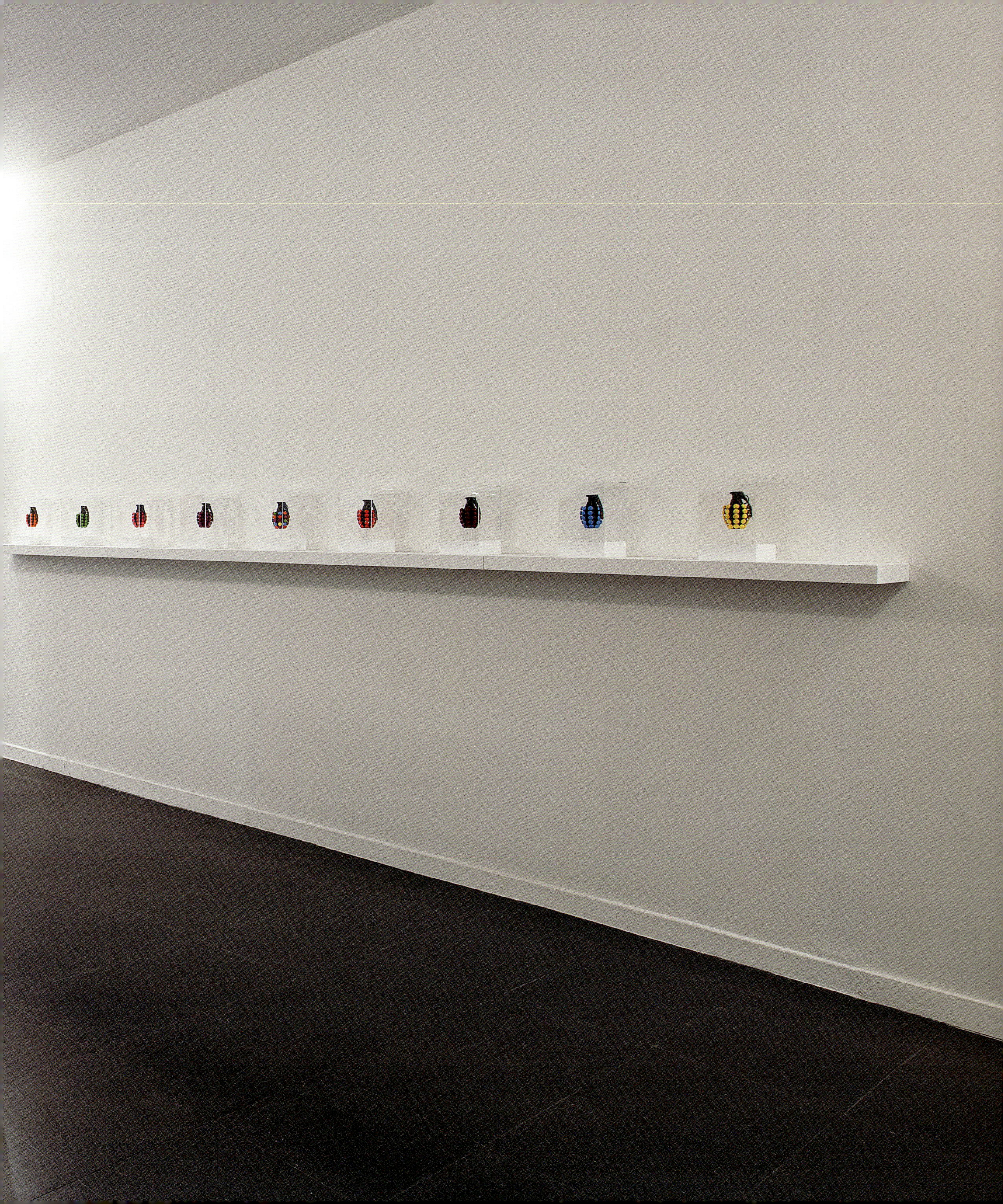

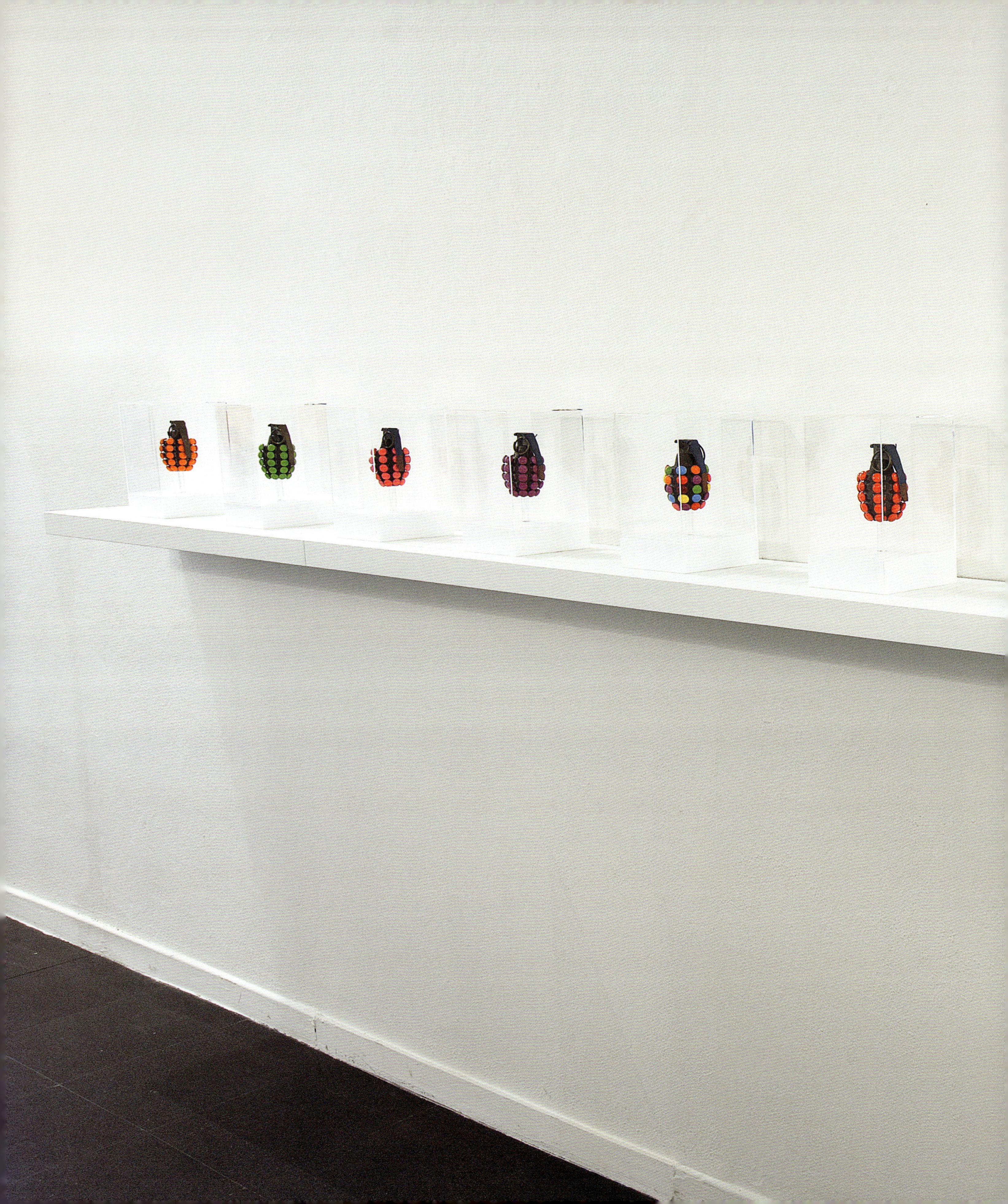

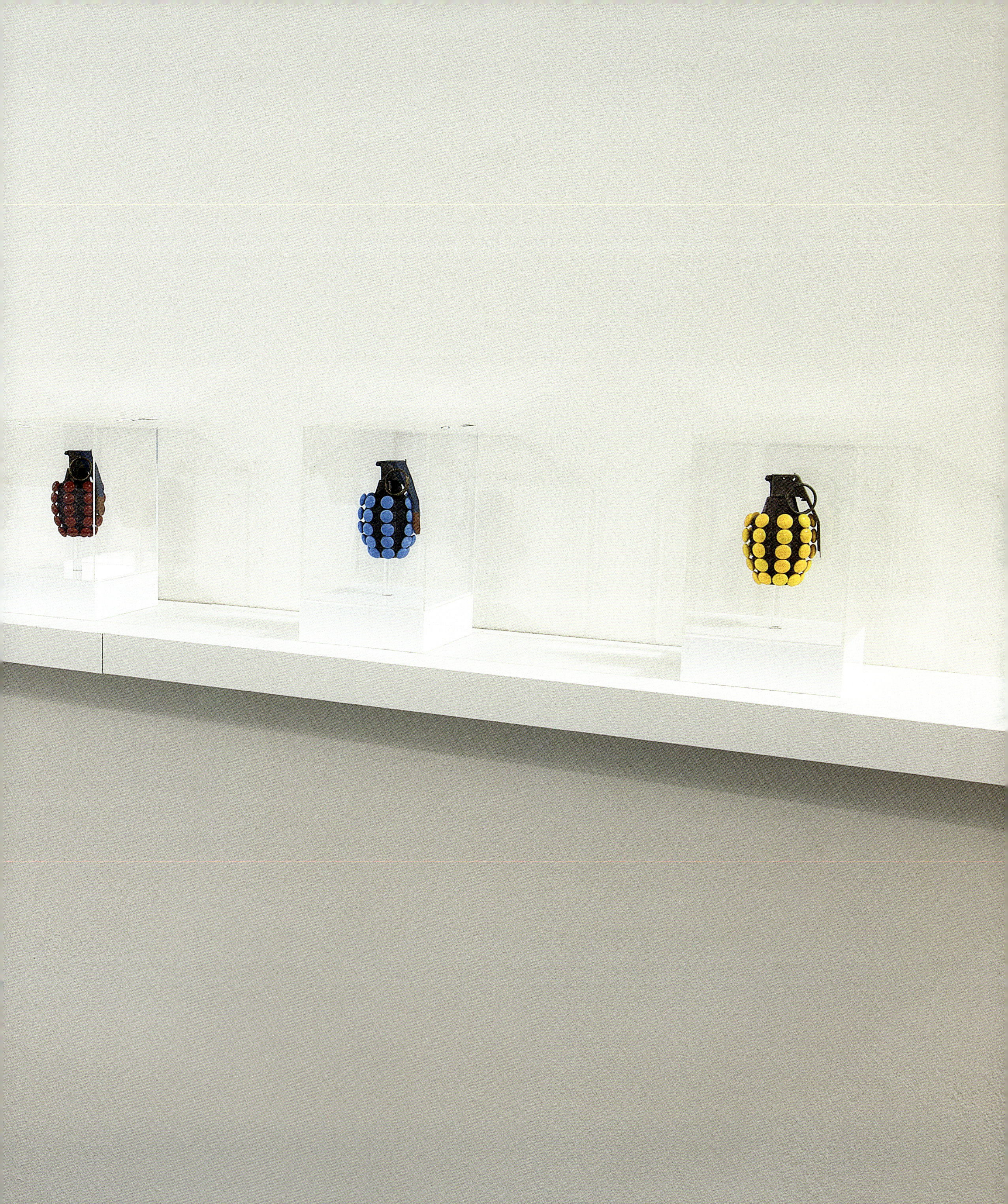

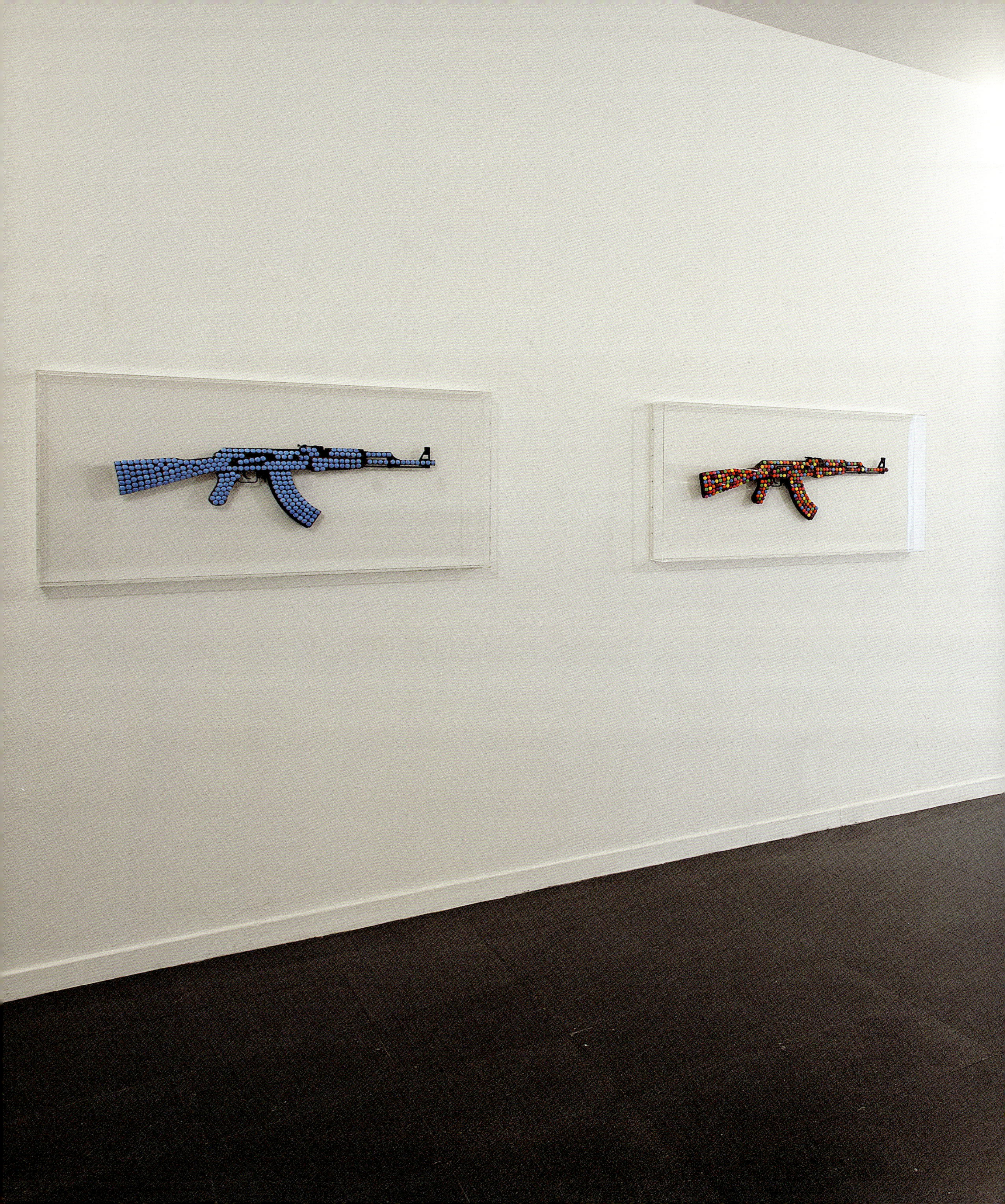

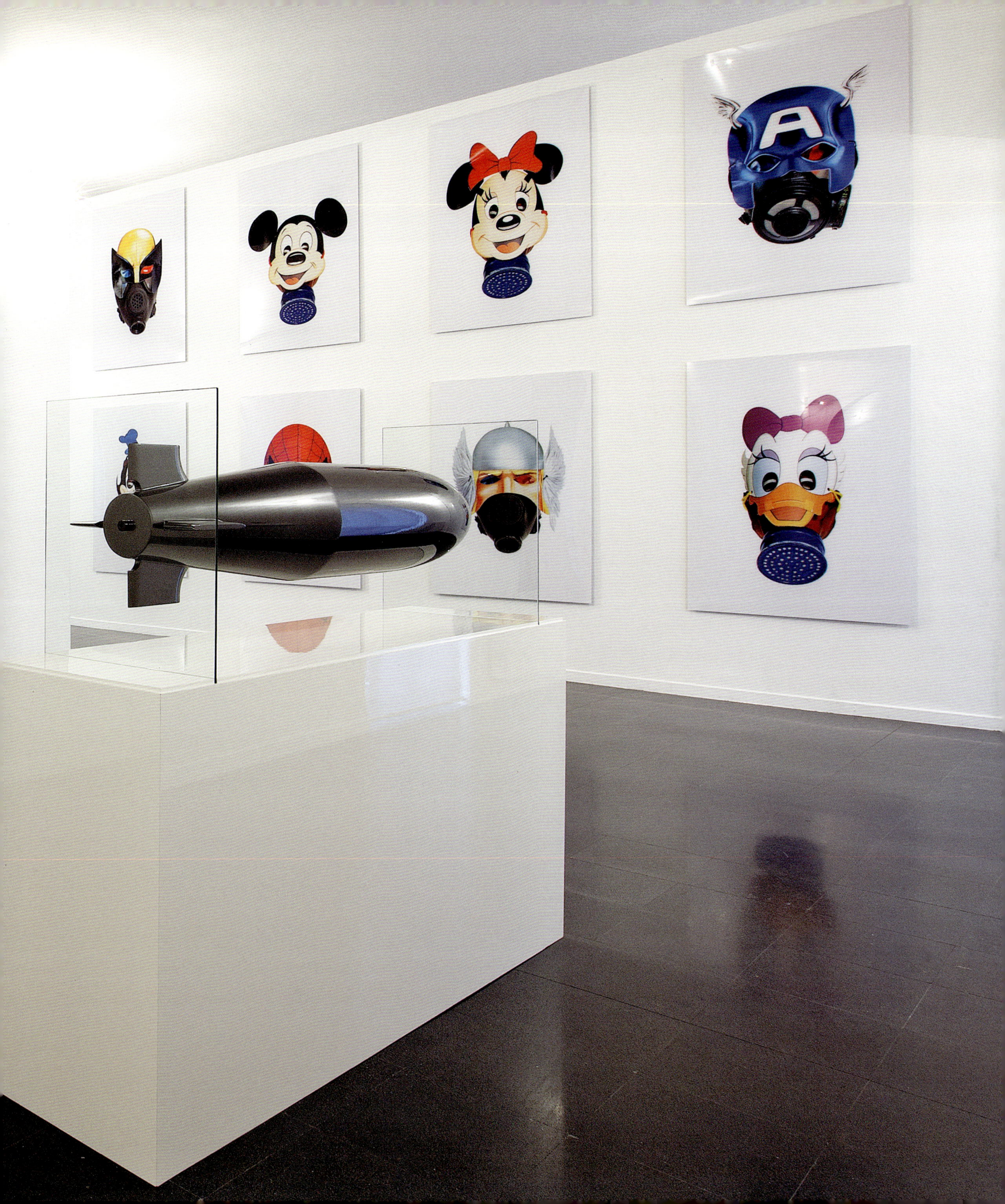

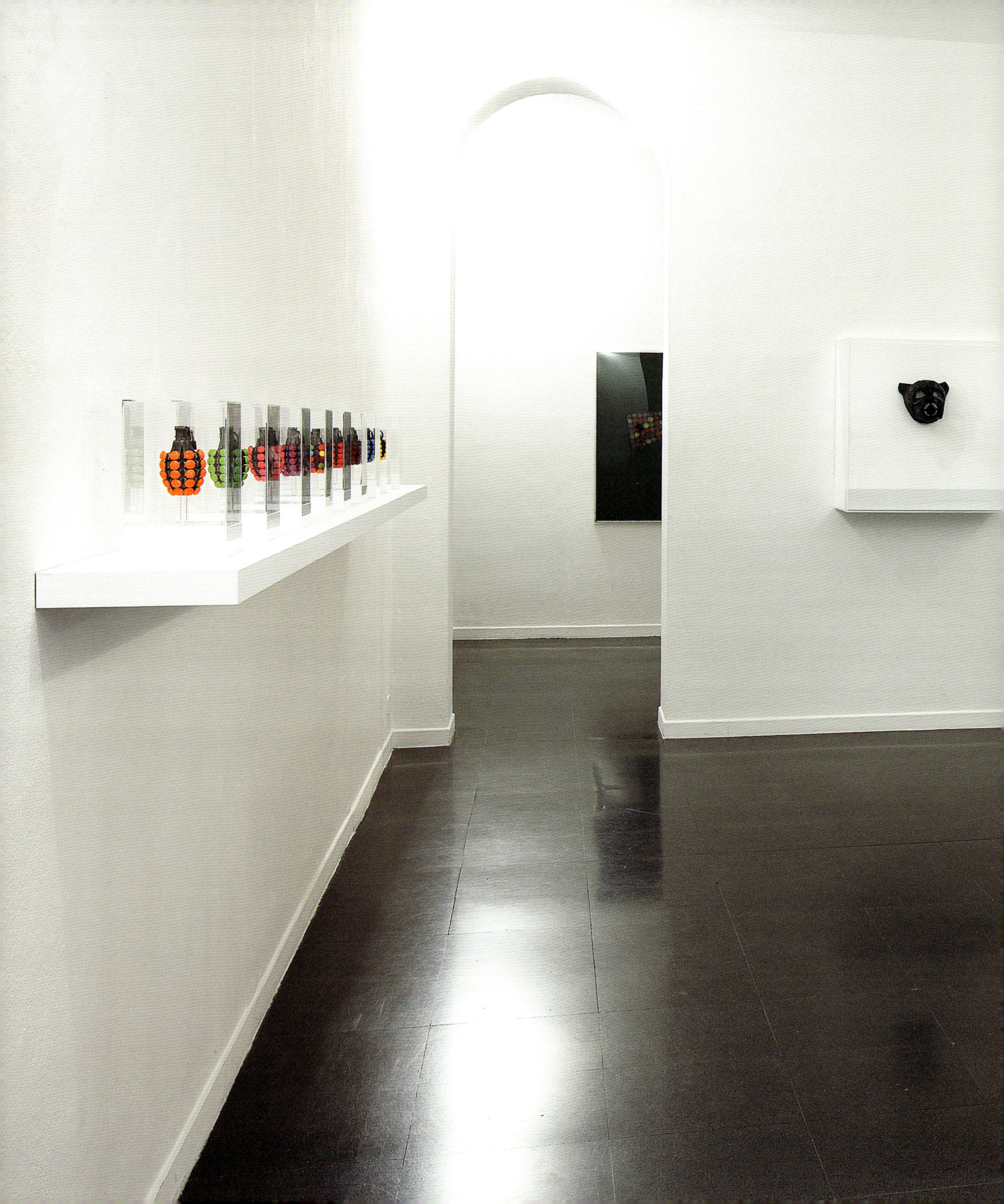

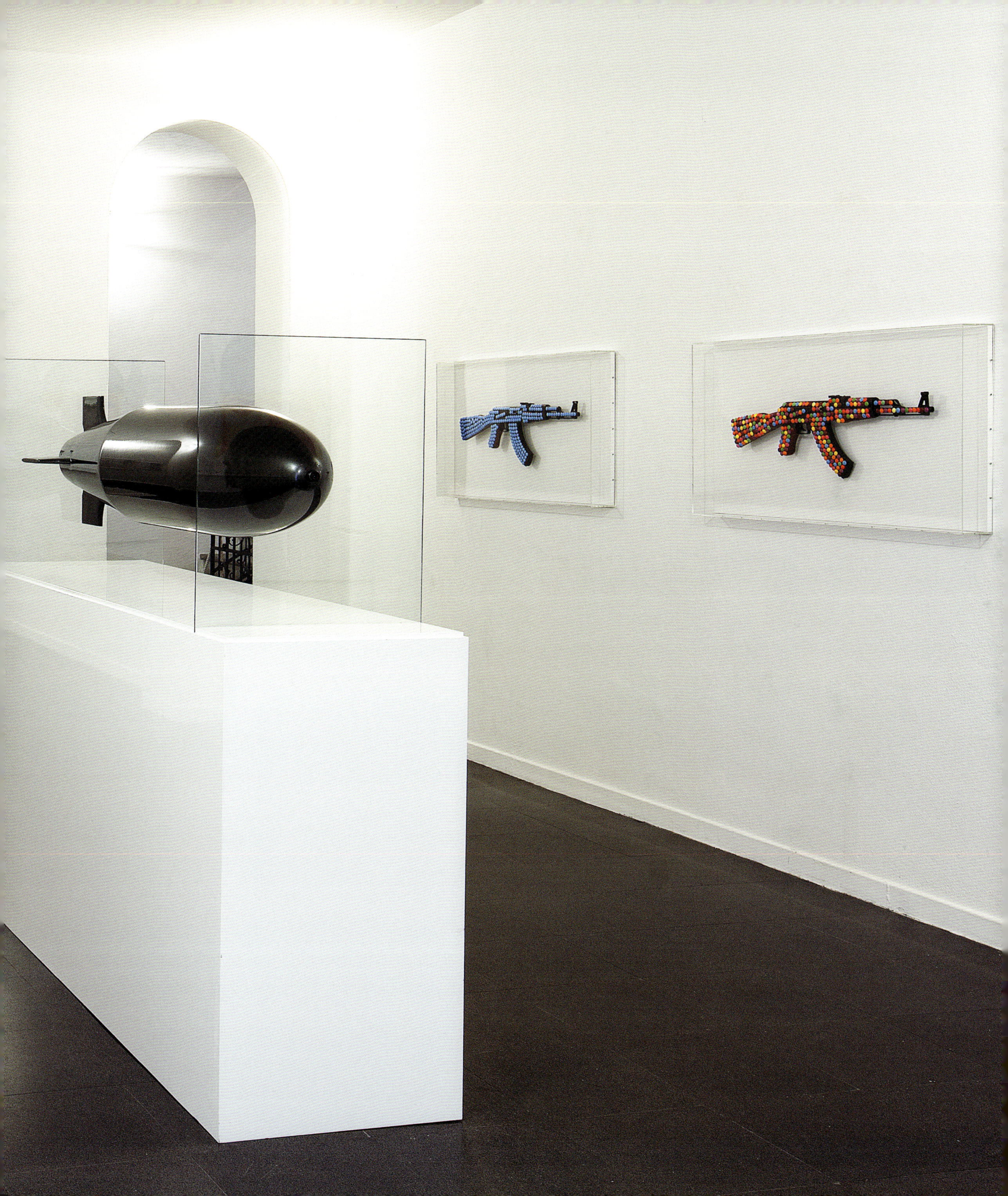

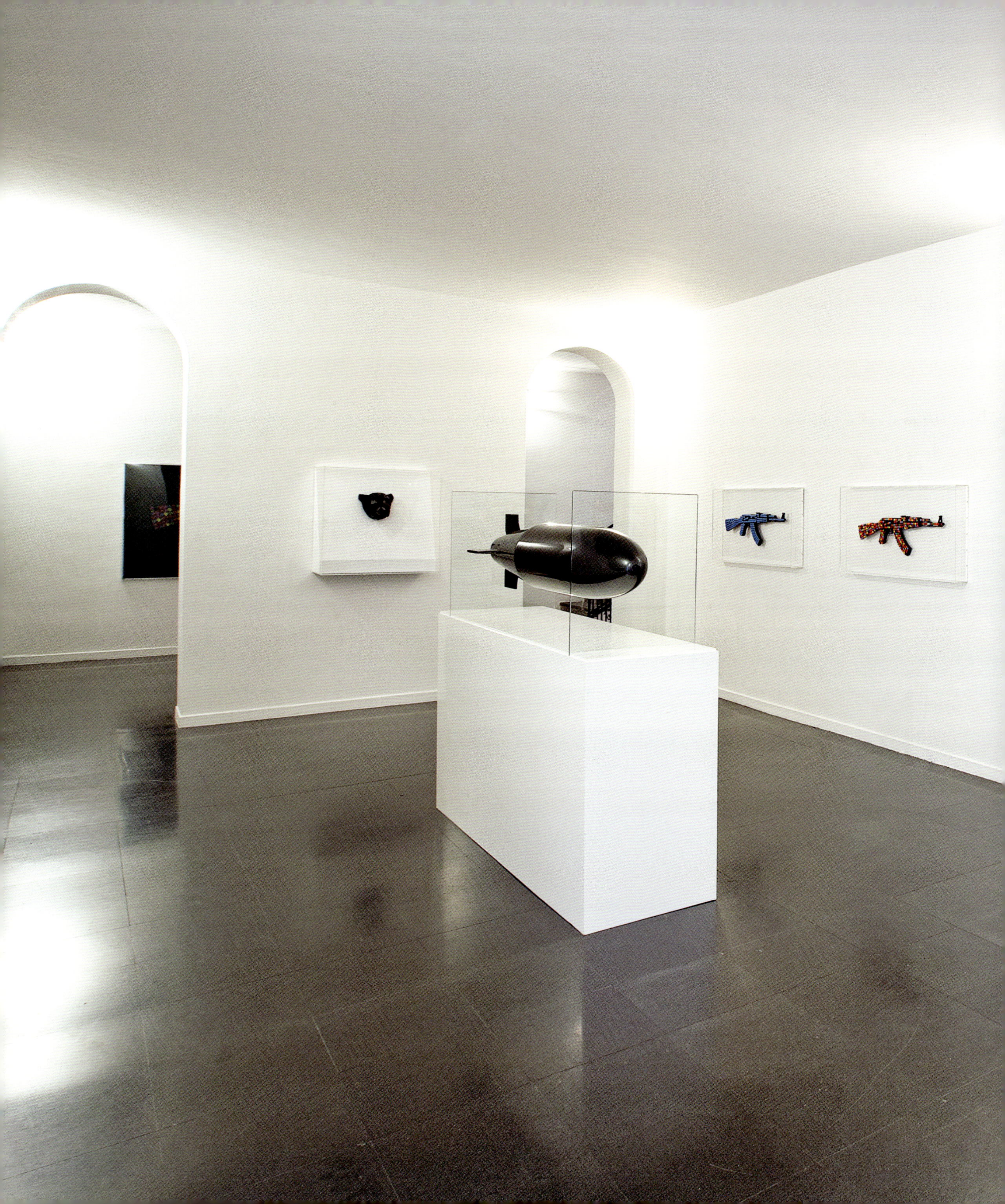

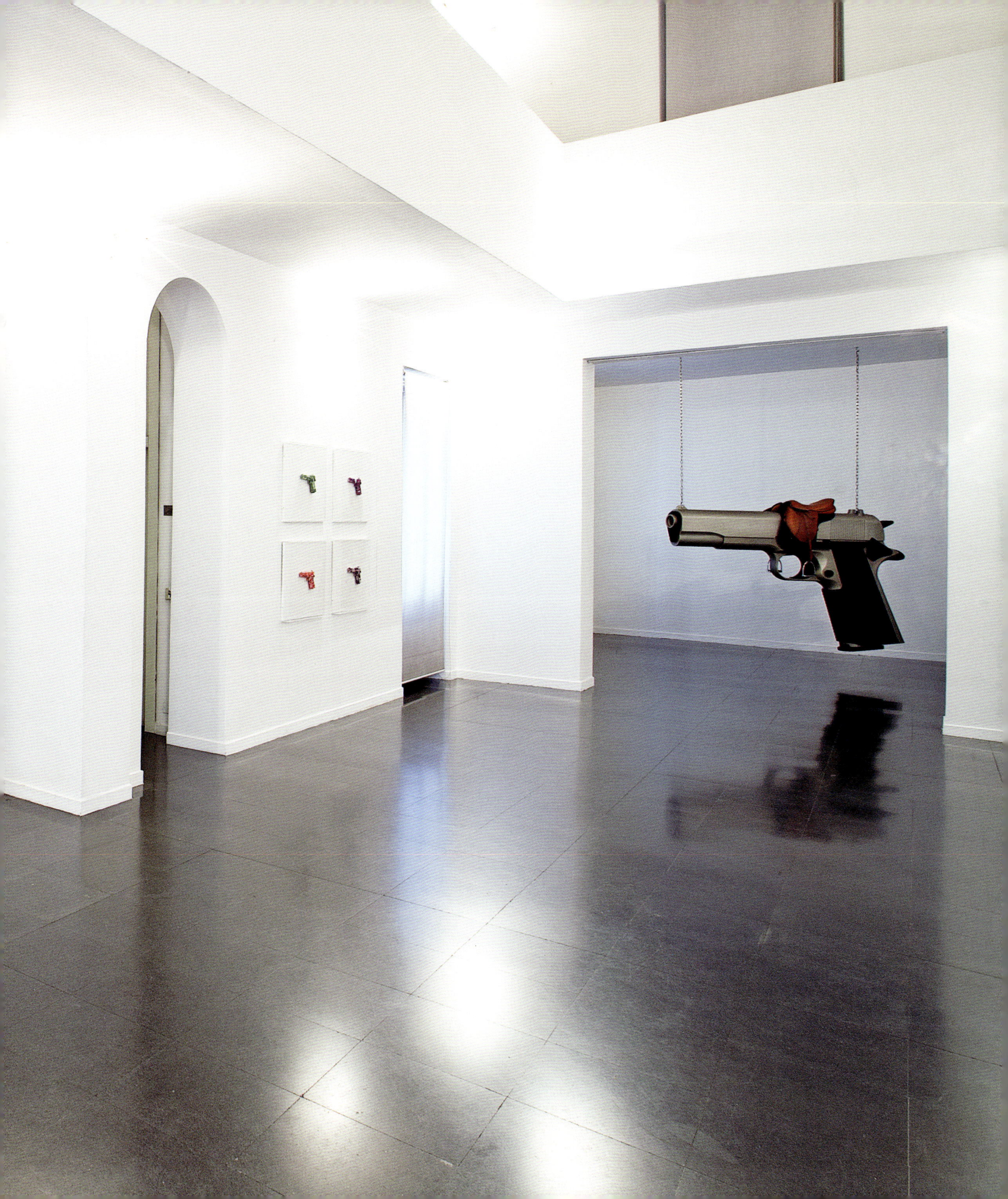

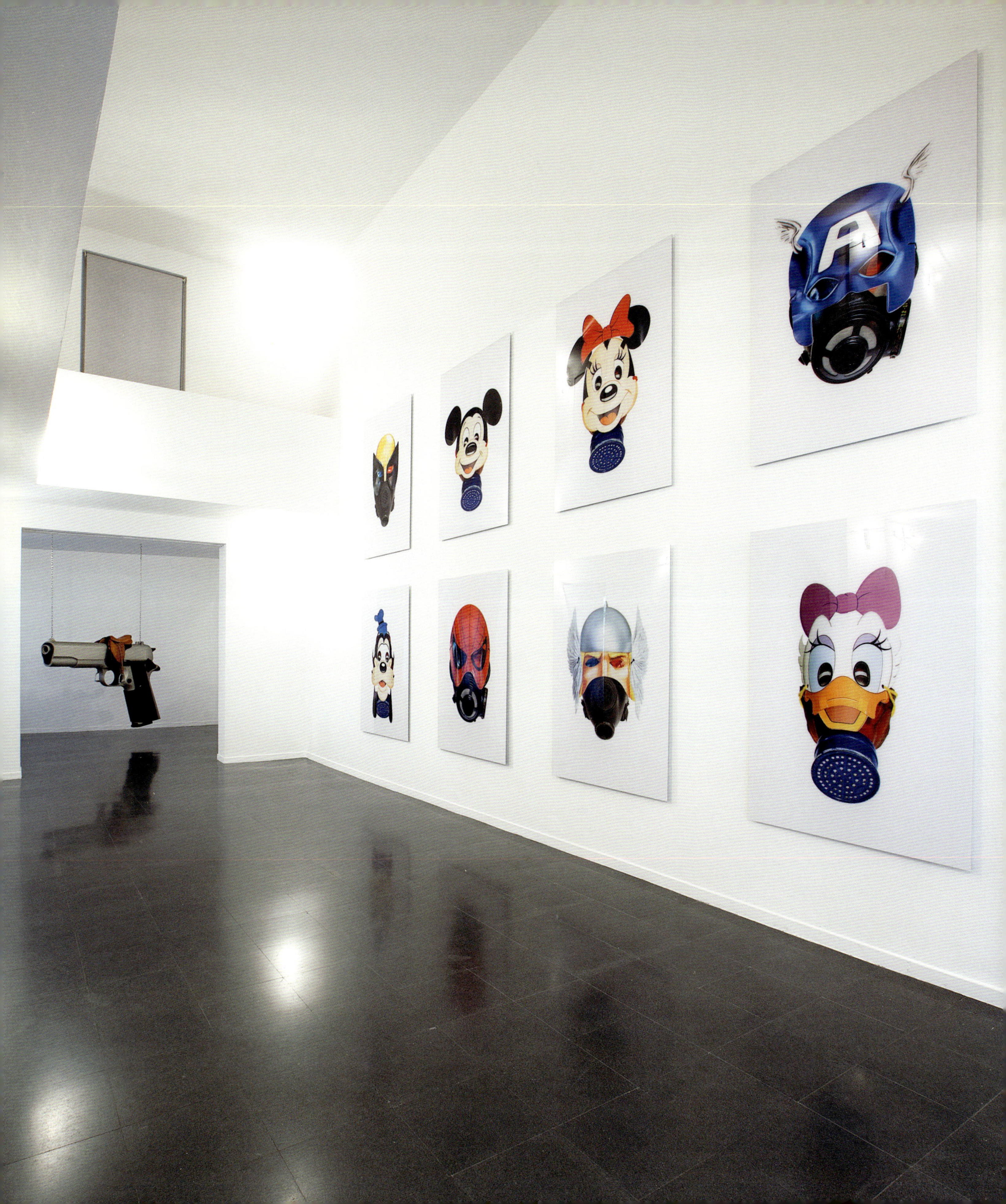

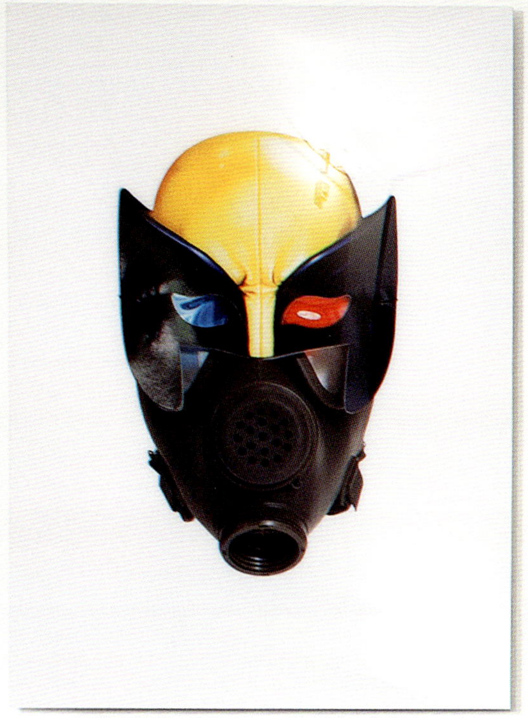
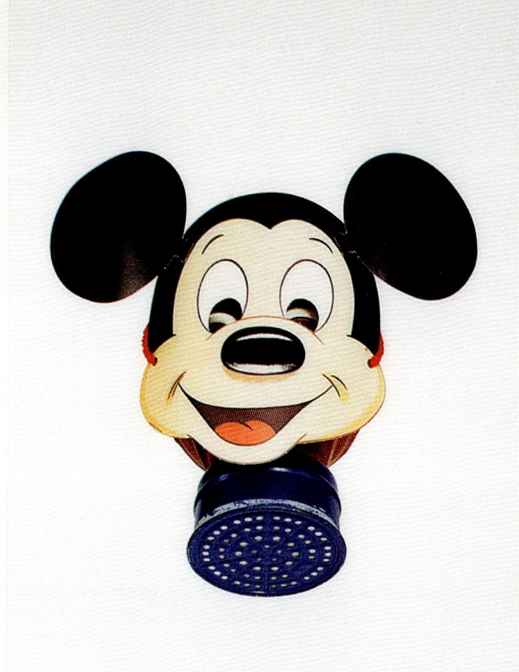
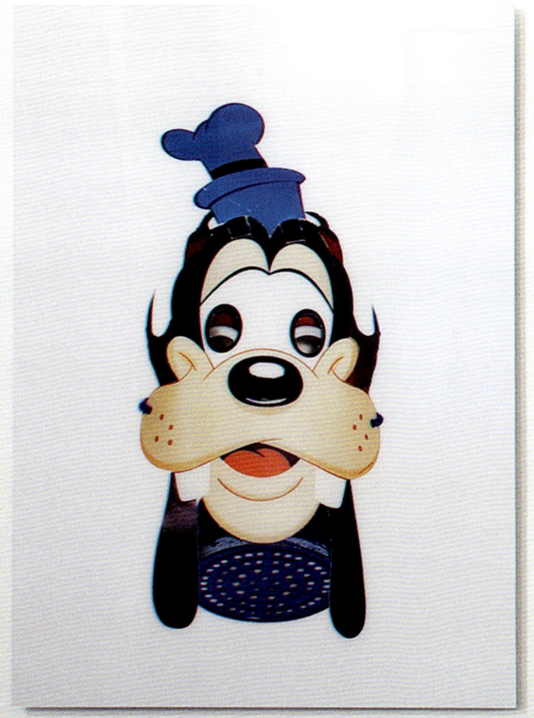
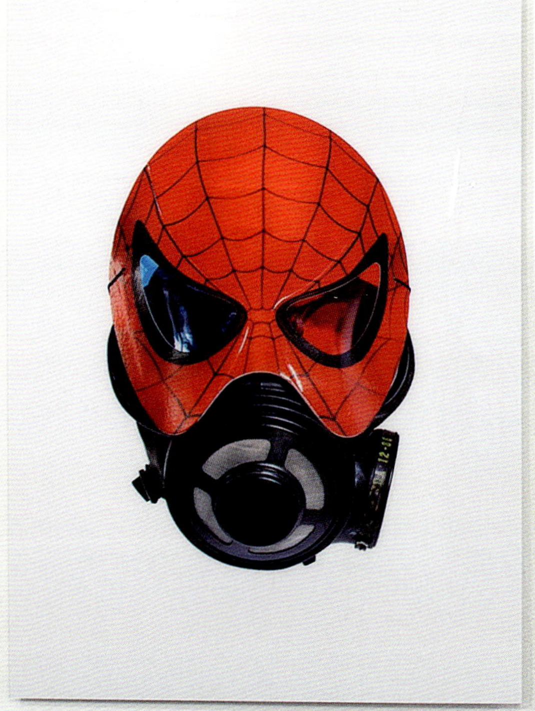

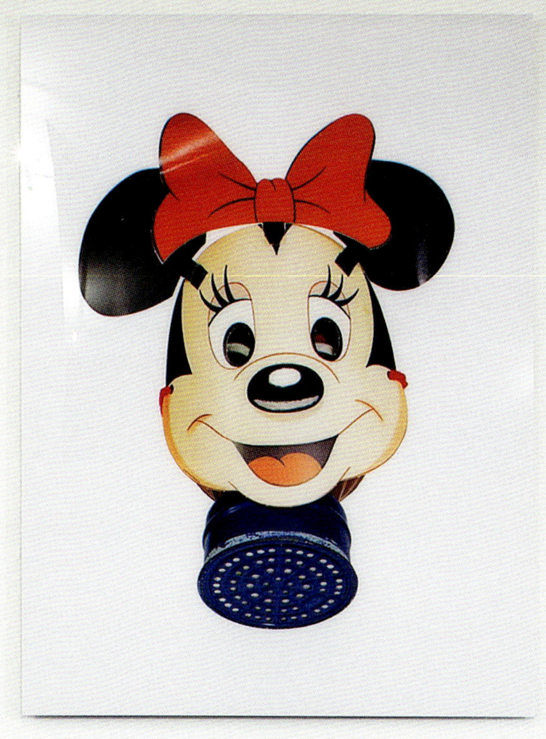
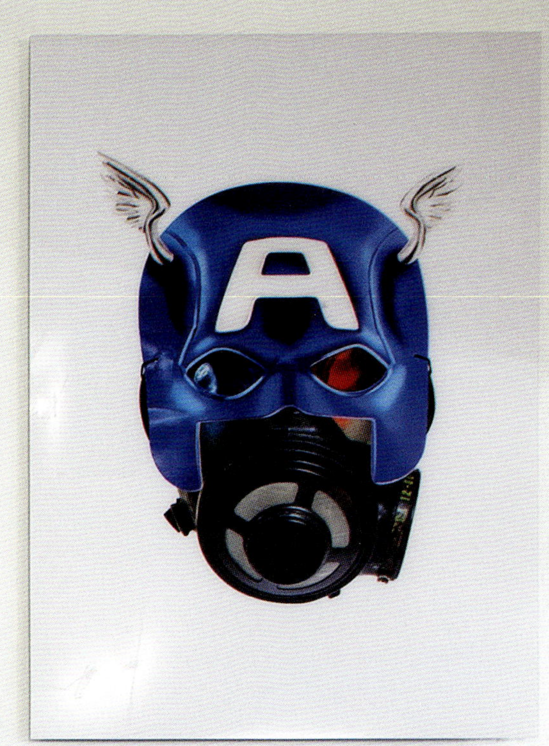
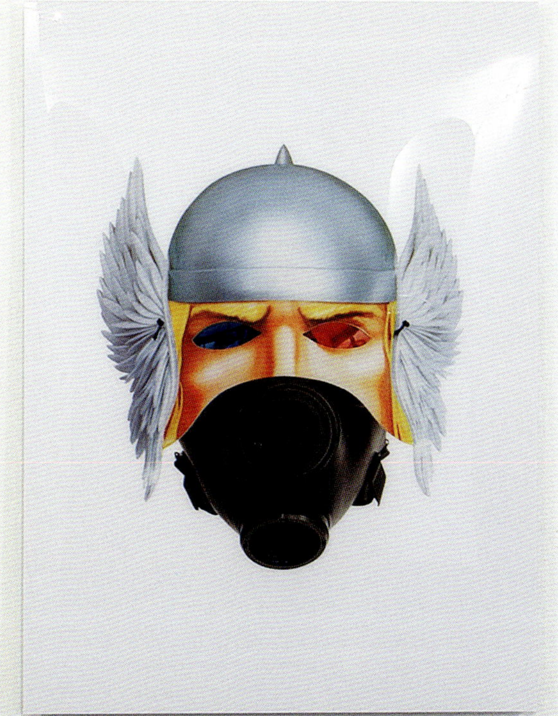
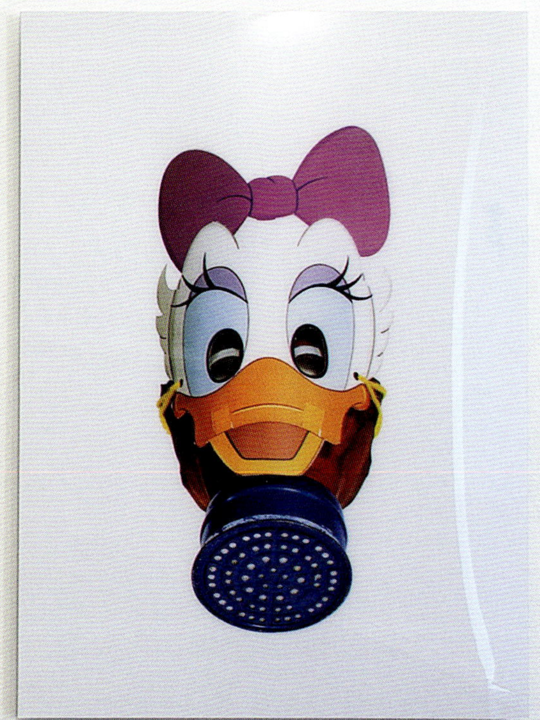

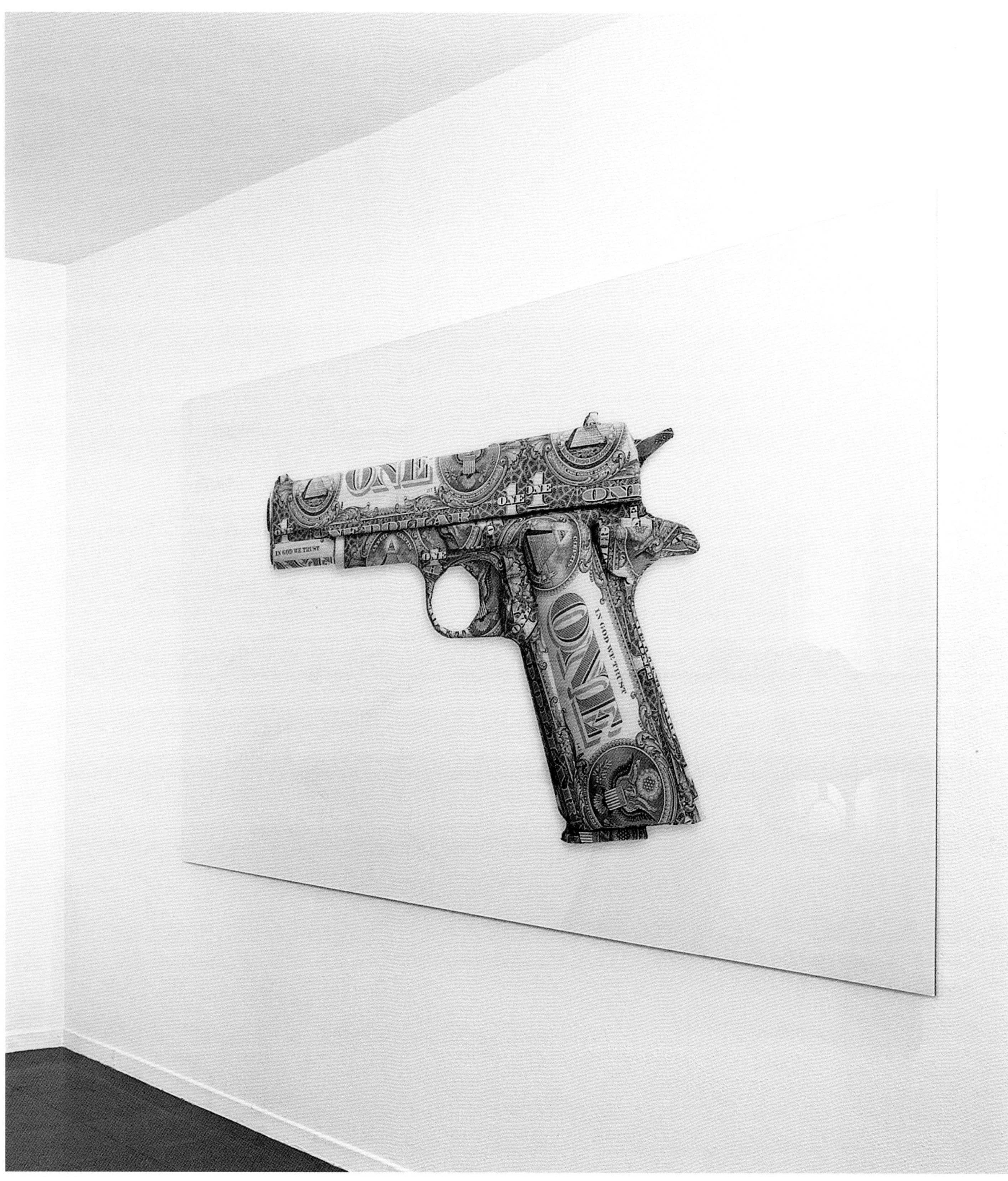

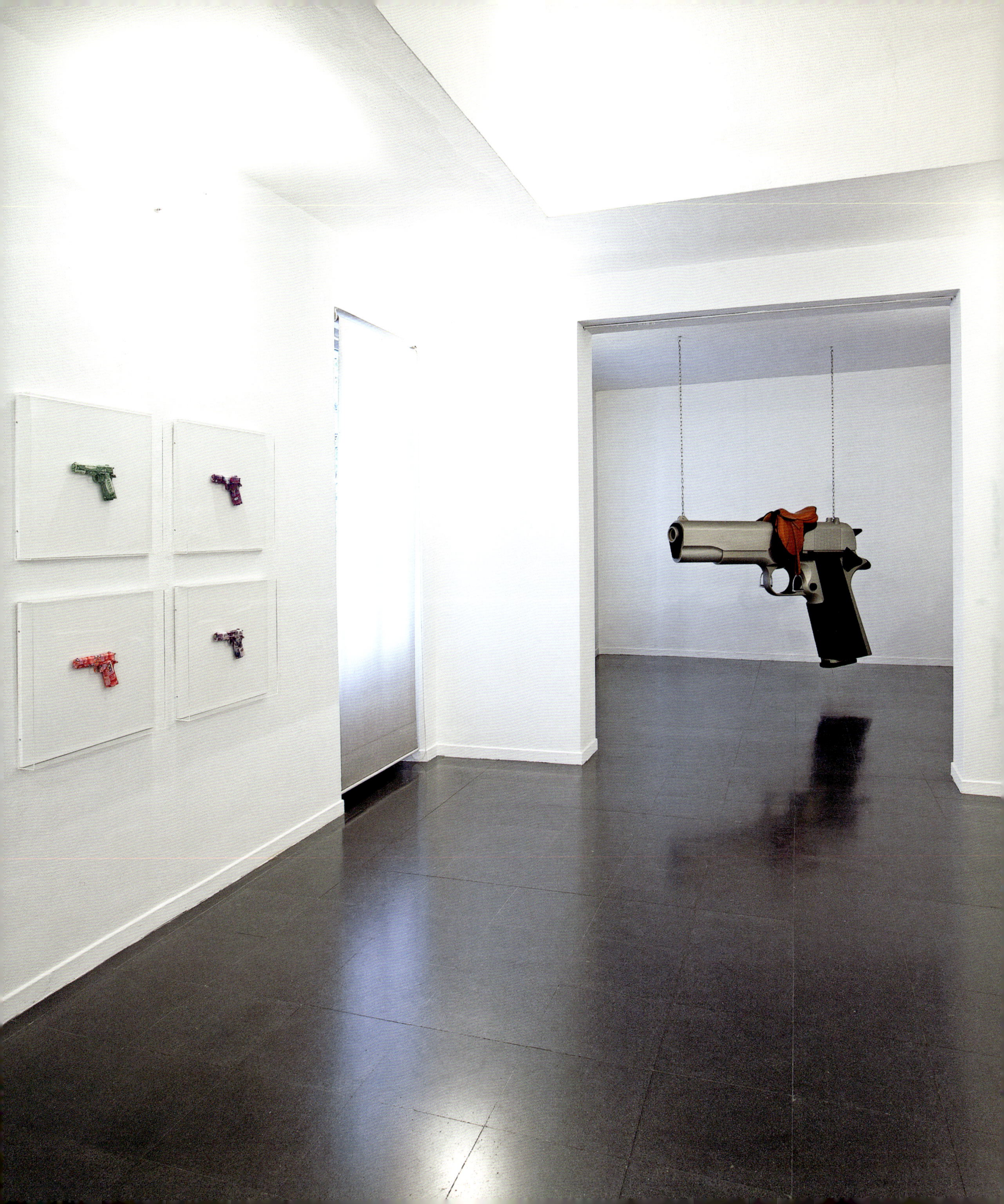

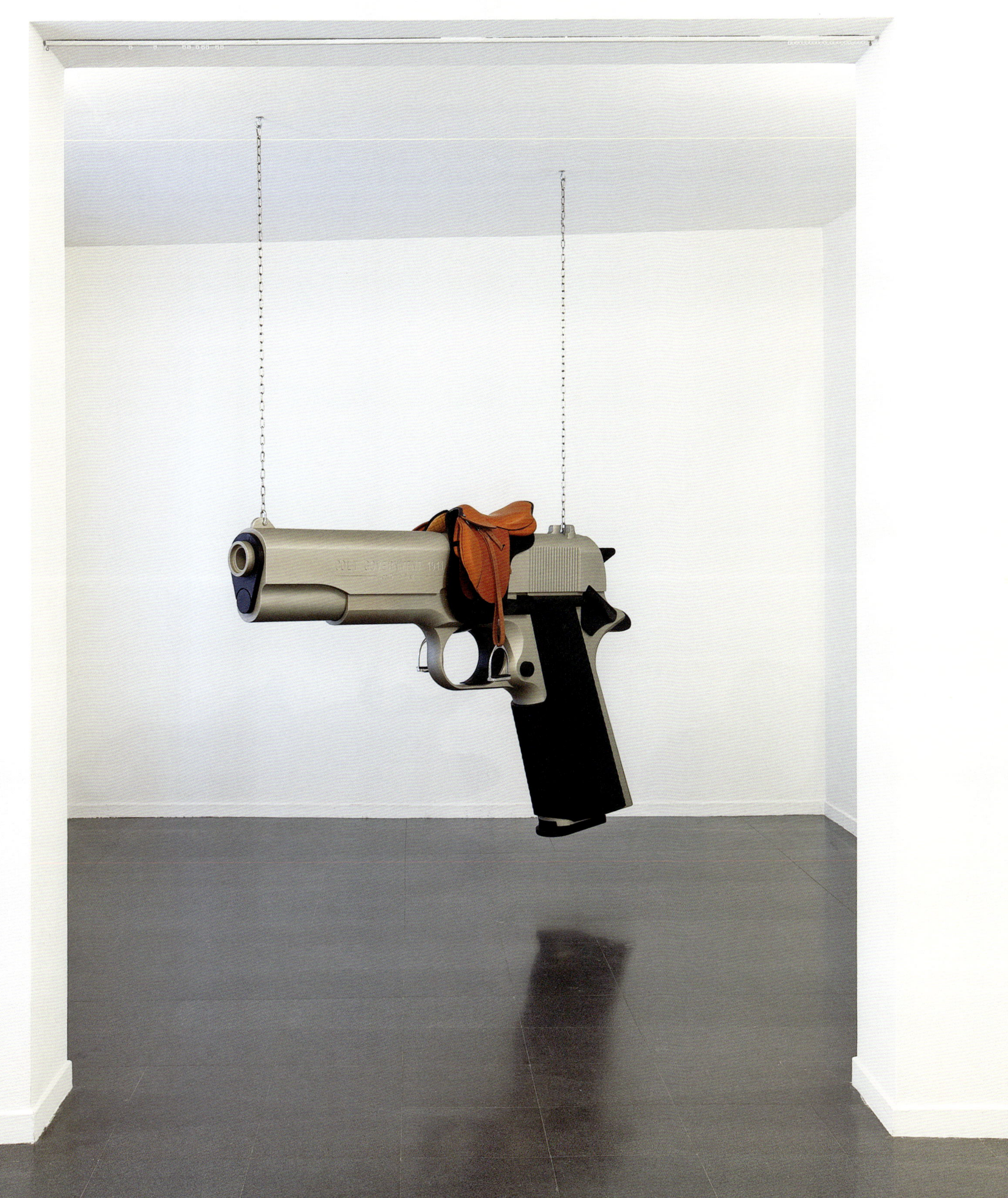

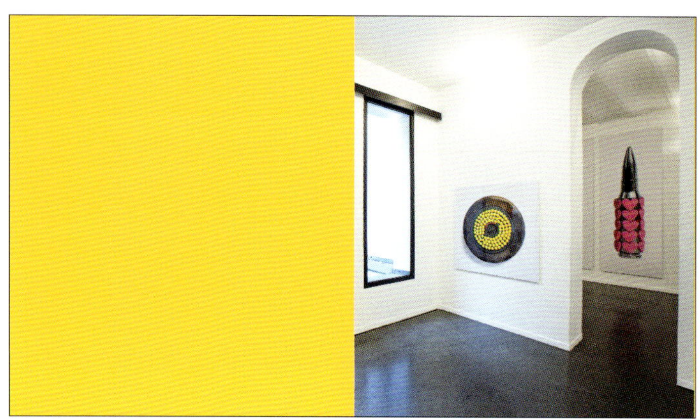

Mine (yellow), 2011
C-Print on diasec
150 x 150 cm

Bullet "Pink Heart", 2011
C-Print on diasec
370 x 123 cm

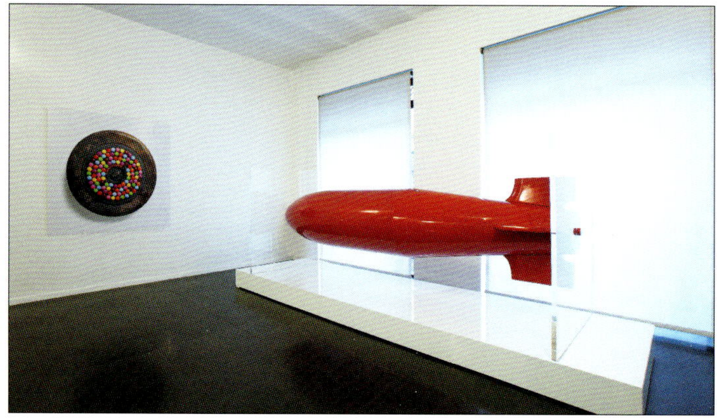

Mine (multicolor), 2009
C-Print on diasec
180 x 180 cm

Chanel 217 (pink bomb), 2011
Synthetic resin, lacquered in
Chanel 217, on wooden base,
mounted on pedestal with Plexiglas
89 x 397 x 89 cm

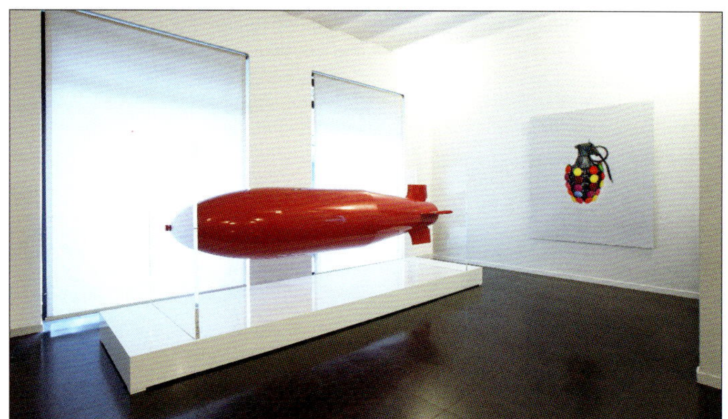

Chanel 217 (pink bomb), 2011
Synthetic resin, lacquered in
Chanel 217, on wooden base,
mounted on pedestal with Plexiglas
89 x 397 x 89 cm

Pineapple (multicolor), 2008
C-Print on diasec
221 x 180 cm

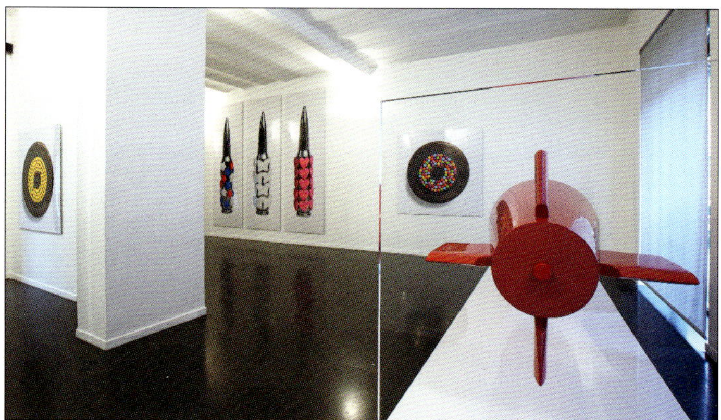

Mine (yellow), 2011
C-Print on diasec
150 x 150 cm

Bullet, 2011
(3 different artworks)
C-Print on diasec
370 x 123 cm each

Mine (multicolor), 2009
C-Print on diasec
180 x 180 cm

Chanel 217 (pink bomb), 2011
Synthetic resin, lacquered in
Chanel 217, on wooden base,
mounted on pedestal with Plexiglas
89 x 397 x 89 cm

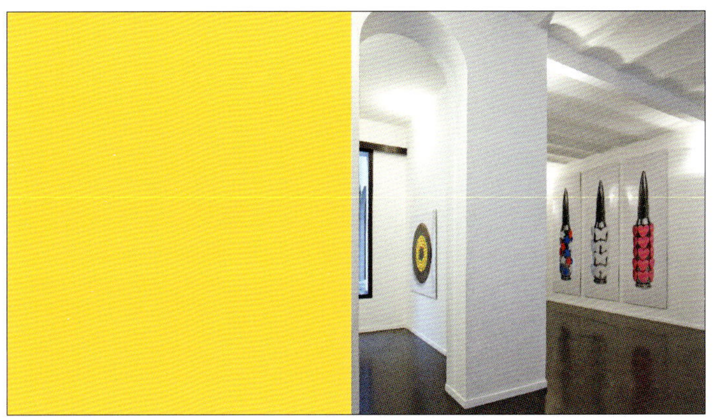

Mine (yellow), 2011
C-Print on diasec
150 x 150 cm

Bullet, 2011
(3 different artworks)
C-Print on diasec
370 x 123 cm each

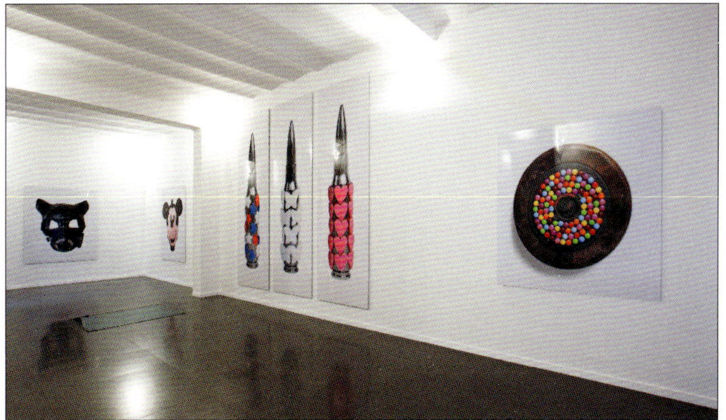

Catwoman, 2011
C-Print on diasec
215 x 180 cm

Mickey, Pearl Harbour 7, 2011
C-Print on diasec
215 x 180 cm

Bullet, 2011
(3 different artworks)
C-Print on diasec
370 x 123 cm each

Mine (multicolor), 2009
C-Print on diasec
180 x 180 cm

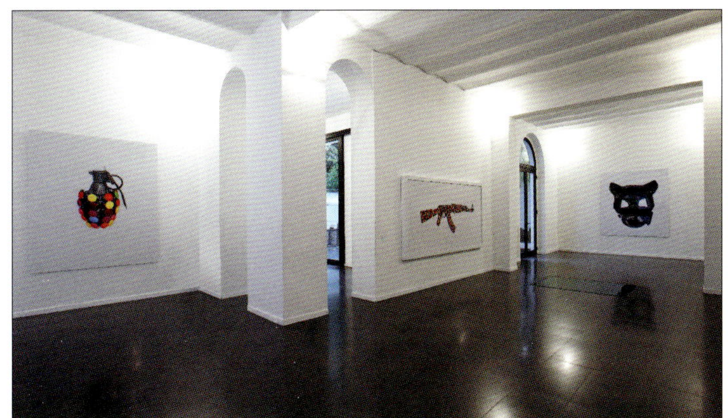

Pineapple (multicolor), 2008
C-Print on diasec
221 x 180 cm

Kalashnikov (multicolor), 2009
C-Print on diasec
155.5 x 300.5 cm (framed)

Catwoman, 2011
C-Print on diasec
215 x 180 cm

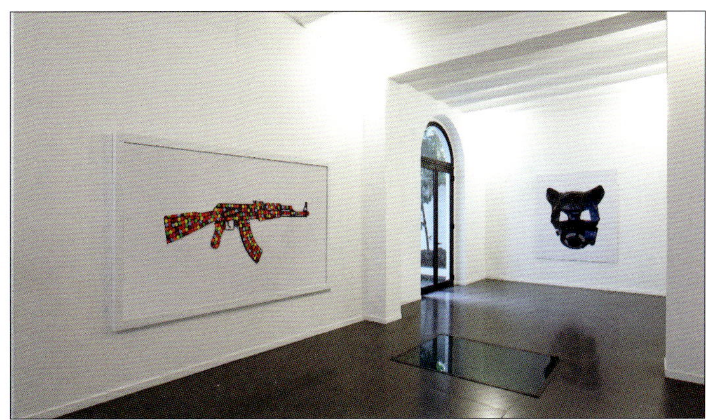

Kalashnikov (multicolor), 2009
C-Print on diasec
155.5 x 300.5 cm (framed)

Catwoman, 2011
C-Print on diasec
215 x 180 cm

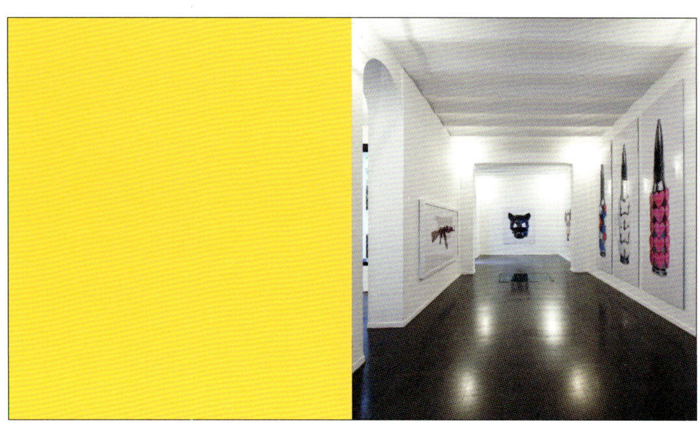

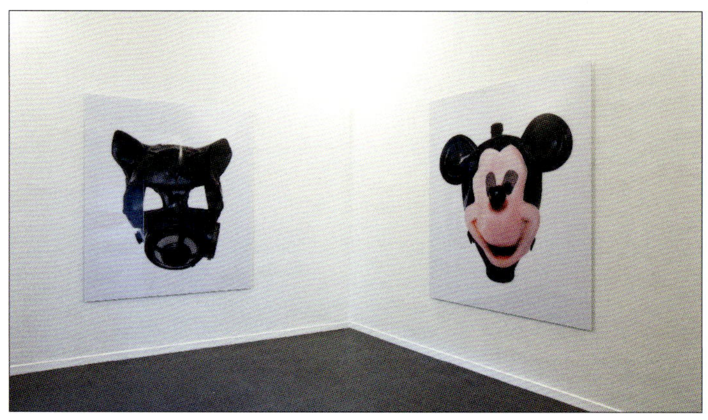

Kalashnikov (multicolor), 2009
C-Print on diasec
155.5 x 300.5 cm (framed)

Catwoman, 2011
C-Print on diasec
215 x 180 cm

Bullet, 2011
(3 different artworks)
C-Print on diasec
370 x 123 cm each

Catwoman, 2011
C-Print on diasec
215 x 180 cm

Mickey, Pearl Harbour 7, 2011
C-Print on diasec
215 x 180 cm

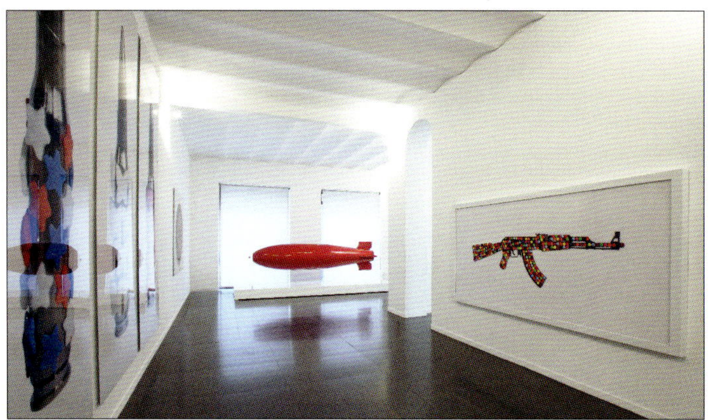

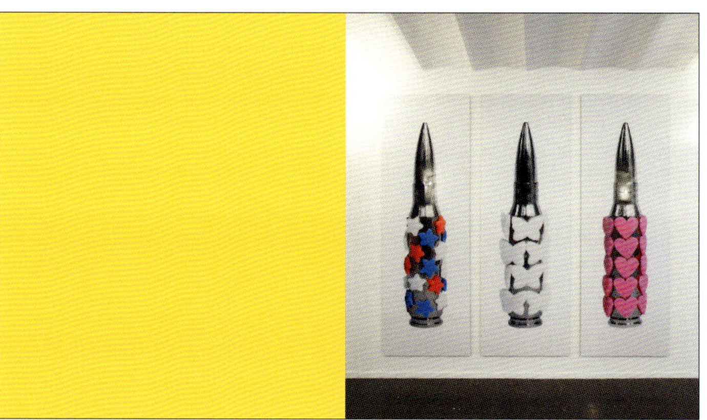

Chanel 217 (pink bomb), 2011
Synthetic resin, lacquered in
Chanel 217, on wooden base,
mounted on pedestal with Plexiglas
89 x 397 x 89 cm

Kalashnikov (multicolor), 2009
C-Print on diasec
155,5 x 300,5 cm (framed)

Bullet "Stars and Stripes", 2011
C-Print on diasec
370 x 123 cm

Bullet "White Butterfly", 2011
C-Print on diasec
370 x 123 cm

Bullet "Pink Heart", 2011
C-Print on diasec
370 x 123 cm

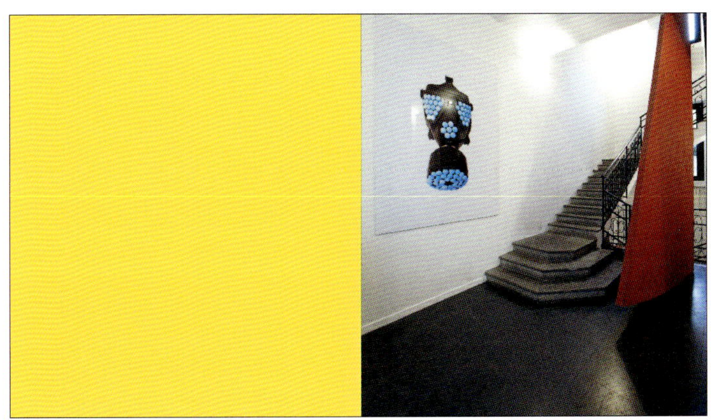

Gas Mask M64 (blue), 2011
C-Print on diasec
250 x 180 cm

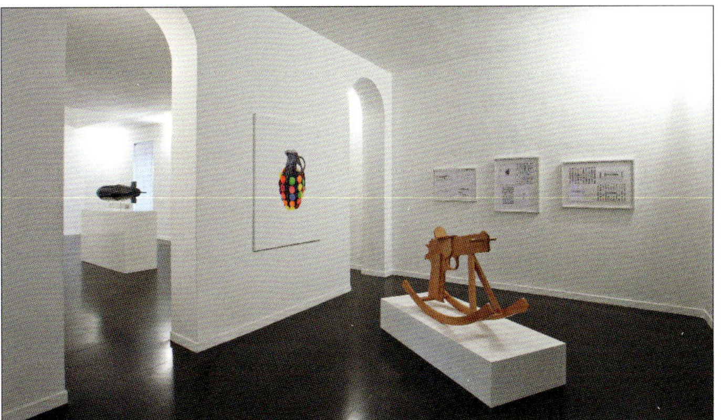

Little Boy (small), 2010
Synthetic resin, lacquered in
original Ferrari Grigio Silverstone
740 WB, on wooden base,
mounted on pedestal with Plexiglas
145 x 200 x 55 cm

Pineapple (multicolor), 2011
Acrylic on canvas
139 x 108 cm

Cheval à bascule, 2011
Beechwood, lacquered
80 x 124 x 39 cm

Drawings (from left)
1. Four colour pencil drawings
on paper, 2008
48.5 x 66.3 cm (framed)
2. Four collages and pencil
drawings on paper, 2007
75.3 x 58.3 cm (framed)
3. Four collages and pencil
drawings on paper, 2007
58.5 x 76.3 cm (framed)

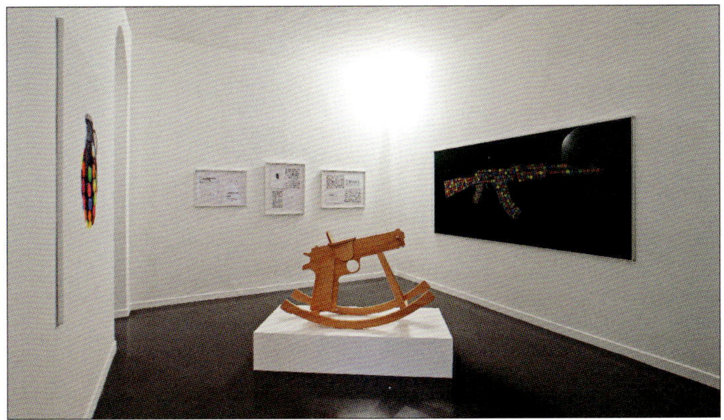

Pineapple (multicolor), 2011
Acrylic on canvas
139 x 108 cm

Cheval à bascule, 2011
Beechwood, lacquered
80 x 124 x 39 cm

Drawings, 2007–08

Kalashnikov (multicolor), 2011
Crayon on chalkboard
121 x 250.4 x 5 cm

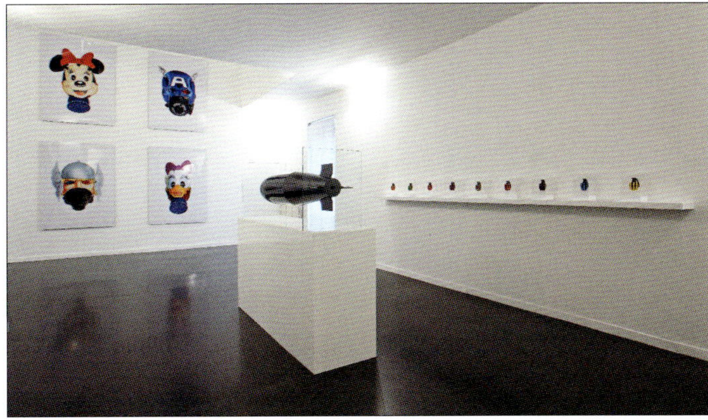

Disney, 2011
(2 different artworks)
C-Print on diasec
174 x 125 cm each

Hero, 2011
(2 different artworks)
C-Print on diasec
174 x 125 cm each

Little Boy (small), 2010
Synthetic resin, lacquered in
original Ferrari Grigio Silverstone
740 WB, on wooden base,
mounted on pedestal with Plexiglas
145 x 200 x 55 cm

Pineapple, 2010
(9 colour variations)
Original grenade with
applicated Smarties, covered
with Plexiglas, on base
25 x 15 x 15 cm each

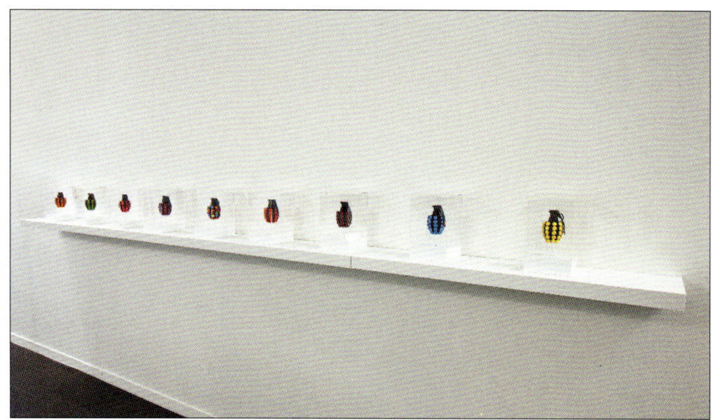

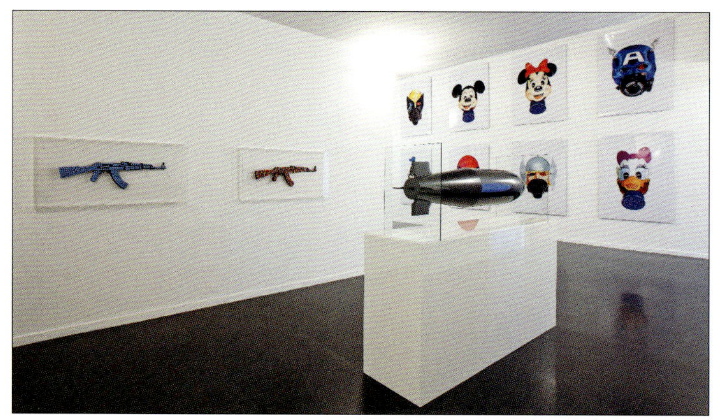

Pineapple, 2010
(9 colour variations)
Original grenade with
applicated Smarties, covered
with Plexiglas, on base
25 x 15 x 15 cm each

Kalashnikov, 2010
(2 colour variations)
Original gun with applicated
Smarties, covered with Plexiglas
61 x 121 x 10.5 cm each

Little Boy (small), 2010
Synthetic resin, lacquered in
original Ferrari Grigio Silverstone
740 WB, on wooden base,
mounted on pedestal with Plexiglas
145 x 200 x 55 cm

Disney, 2011
(4 different artworks)
C-Print on diasec
174 x 125 cm each

Hero, 2011
(4 different artworks)
C-Print on diasec
174 x 125 cm each

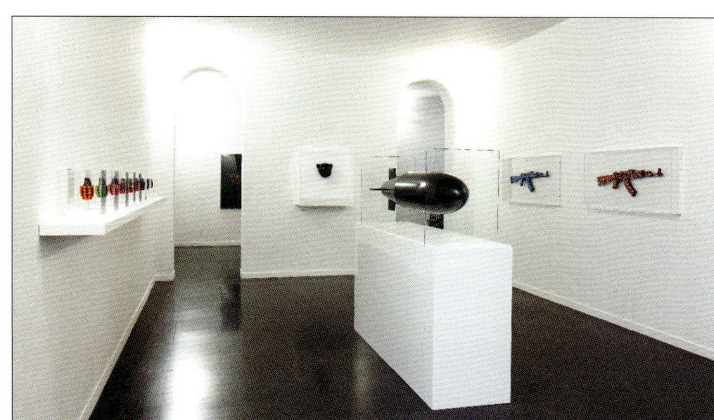

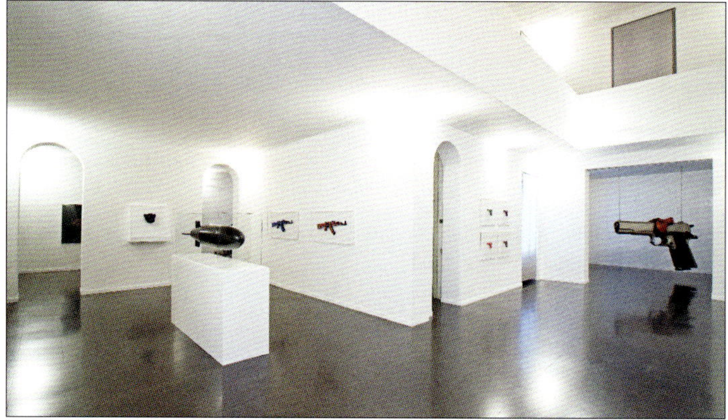

Pineapple, 2010
(9 colour variations)
Original grenade with
applicated Smarties, covered
with Plexiglas, on base
25 x 15 x 15 cm each

Catwoman, 2011
Mask on gas mask,
covered with Plexiglas
80 x 80 x 40 cm

Little Boy (small), 2010
Synthetic resin, lacquered in
original Ferrari Grigio Silverstone
740 WB, on wooden base,
mounted on pedestal with Plexiglas
145 x 200 x 55 cm

Kalashnikov, 2010
(2 colour variations)
Original gun with applicated
Smarties, covered with Plexiglas
61 x 121 x 10.5 cm each

Catwoman, 2011
Mask on gas mask,
covered with Plexiglas
80 x 80 x 40 cm

Little Boy (small), 2010
Synthetic resin, lacquered in
original Ferrari Grigio Silverstone
740 WB, on wooden base,
mounted on pedestal with Plexiglas
145 x 200 x 55 cm

Kalashnikov, 2010
(2 colour variations)
Original gun with applicated
Smarties, covered with Plexiglas
61 x 121 x 10.5 cm each

Government US Dollar, 2010
Government 10
Hong Kong Dollar, 2011
*Government 100 Renminbi
Yuan,* 2011
Government 500 Rubel, 2011
Original guns, coated with
banknotes, covered with Plexiglas
58 x 68 x 7 cm each

Government Balançoir, 2011
Synthetic resin, metal lacquered,
original saddle (Hermès, orange)
153 x 237 x 37 cm

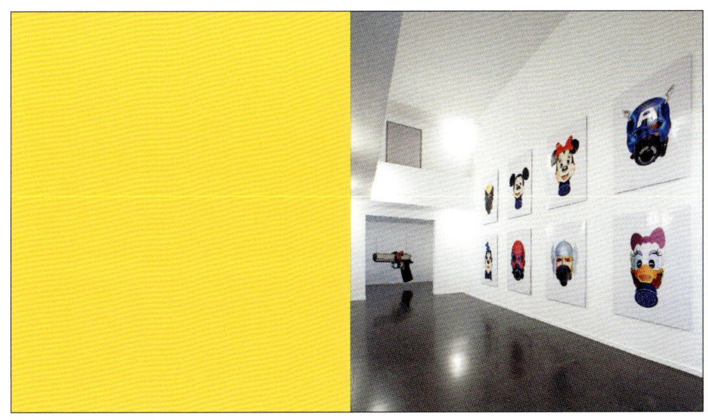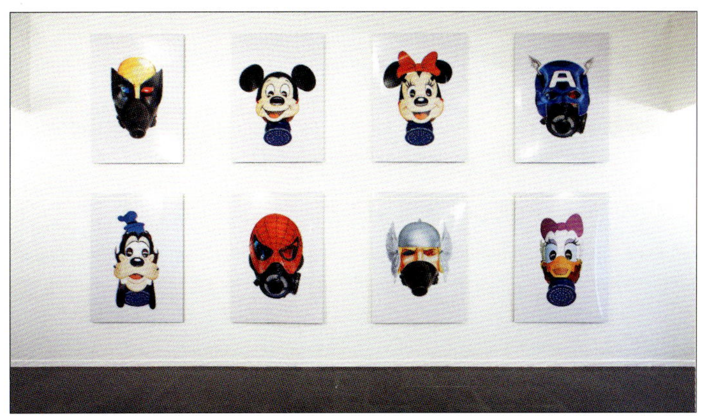

Government Balançoir, 2011
Synthetic resin, metal lacquered,
original saddle (Hermès, orange)
153 x 237 x 37 cm

Hero, 2011
(4 different artworks)
C-Print on diasec
174 x 125 cm each

Disney, 2011
(4 different artworks)
C-Print on diasec
174 x 125 cm each

Hero, 2011
(from top left: Wolverine, Captain
America, Spiderman Red and Thor)
C-Print on diasec
174 x 125 cm

Disney, 2011
(from top left: Mickey,
Minnie, Goofy and Daisy)
C-Print on diasec
174 x 125 cm each

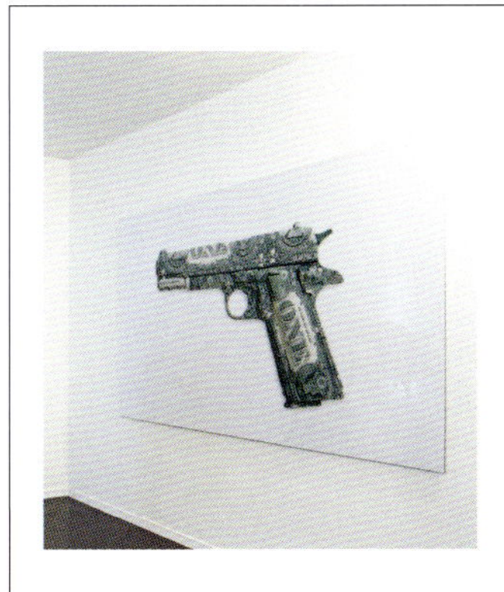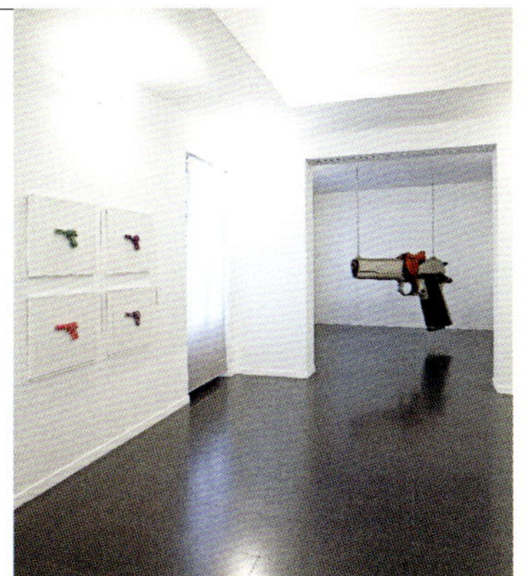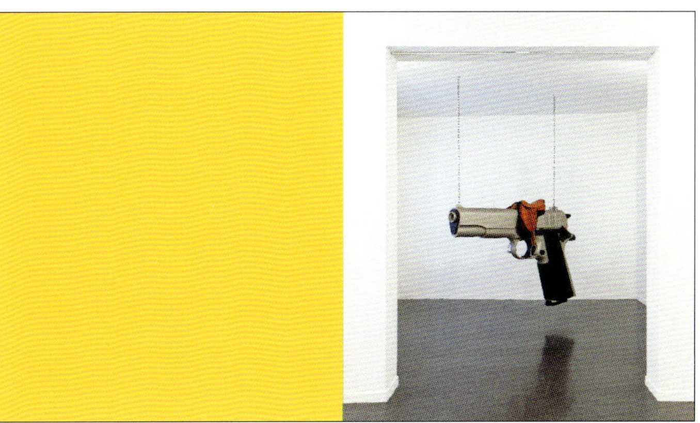

Government US Dollar, 2011
C-Print on diasec
180 x 300 cm

Government US Dollar, 2010
*Government 10
Hong Kong Dollar*, 2011
*Government 100 Renminbi
Yuan*, 2011
Government 500 Rubel, 2011
Original guns, coated with
banknotes, covered with Plexiglas
58 x 68 x 7 cm each

Government Balançoir, 2011
Synthetic resin, metal lacquered,
original saddle (Hermès, orange)
153 x 237 x 37 cm

Government Balançoir, 2011
Synthetic resin, metal lacquered,
original saddle (Hermès, orange)
153 x 237 x 37 cm

Kata Legrady was born in Hungary. Youth champion in gymnastics, she also received a musical and aesthetic education. She studied at the Conservatory of Music in Pécs as lyric opera singer. In Budapest, she studied drama at Gor Nagy Maria Drama School and participated in different musical and film projects. For several years in Germany she taught piano and singing and conducted the Choir Sinfonia of Hanover. While living in Oxford, New York and Paris, she started to visit various artist's studios and made the acquaintance of Jacques Villeglé, Raymond Hains and Philippe Pasqua, among others. In 2004, she met Daniel Spoerri who became a friend and mentor of her artistic activities. Her public artistic life started in 2010. She now lives and works in Hanover, Paris and Budapest.

Kata Legrady's works are regularly shown in main international art fairs, among which: Art Paris Art Fair 2010 to 2013, Grand Palais, Paris, in collaboration with Galerie Rabouan Moussion; Art HK, Hong Kong International Art Fair 2012, Hong Kong, in collaboration with Pékin Fine Arts; The Armory Show 2013, Piers 92 & 94, New York City, in collaboration with Pékin Fine Arts; Drawing Now 2013, Carrousel du Louvre, Paris, in collaboration with Galerie Rabouan Moussion; Art Basel Hong Kong 2013, Hong Kong, in collaboration with Pékin Fine Arts.

Selected exhibitions

2010
Bombs and Candies, Galerie Rabouan Moussion, Paris (solo exhibition).
2011
Kata Legrady, Galerie Pari Nadimi, Toronto (solo exhibition).
Masks and Guns, Galerie Rabouan Moussion, Paris (solo exhibition).
Le Cabinet de Curiosités de Thomas Erber, Browns, London.
Kata Legrady, Fondazione Mudima, Milan (solo exhibition).
2012
Bombs and Candies – dulce et decorum, Denkerei Bazon Brock, Berlin (solo exhibition).
Le Luxe, mode d'emploi, Passage de Retz, Paris.
Le Cabinet de Curiosités de Thomas Eber, Andreas Murkudis, Berlin.
Le Cabinet de Curiosités de Thomas Erber, special edition, BMW George V, Paris.
2013
Bombs and Candies, Kulturstiftung Marienmünster, Marienmünster (solo exhibition).
Hybride 2, Ancien hôpital général, Douai.
Kata Legrady & Wang Luyan, Hong Kong Arts Centre, Hong Kong.
2014
Caravana Negra, La Boca, Buenos Aires.
Kata Legrady, ZKM | Zentrum für Kunst und Medientechnologie Karlsruhe (solo exhibition).
Kata Legrady, Käthe-Kollwitz-Museum, Berlin.

Selected literature
Bombs and Candies (Milan: Skira editore, 2011).
Kata Legrady (Milan: Skira editore, 2013).
Kata Legrady Drawings (Milan: Skira editore, 2013).
Kata Legrady (Berlin: Distanz Verlag, 2013).

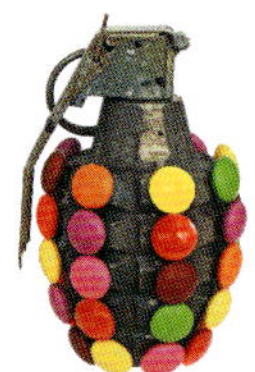